MW00424596

EMPTY, EMPTY. HAPPY, HAPPY.

The Essential Teachings of a Simple Monk

—

TYLER LEWKE

Second Edition

For the happiness of the many.

MY WISH
BY SHANTIDEVA

*May I become at all times, both now and forever, a protector
for those without protection, a guide for those who have
lost their way, a ship for those with an ocean to cross,
a sanctuary for those in danger, a lamp for those without light,
a place of refuge for those who lack shelter and a servant
to those in need. By means of these meritorious deeds,
may I never join with the unwise, only the wise, until the time
I obtain Nirvana.*

"SIMPLE TEACHINGS OFTEN HAVE THE MOST DEPTH"
–BHANTE SUJATHA

1. We must learn to live in truth as it always outlasts falsehood.

2. Words without actions are just empty sounds.

3. Don't let your heart become blind by relying on your eyes to see beauty.

4. When you are truly honest, kind and moral, all beings can sense it even before you speak or act.

5. You will have to rely on yourself. Teachers guide the way, friends give support, life is the opportunity. How you do the work is up to you.

6. Love is only a word until it is put into action.

7. Every moment we are losing whatever belongs to us.

8. Do everything without expectation, then witness as you receive everything you need.

9. Love is not fake, people make it seem so.

10. Loneliness is challenging but the moment you feel the beauty of it, you no longer depend on another human being.

11. Life is simple: do not harm yourself or others.

12. Be simple. Think deeply.

13. Death teaches us the importance of being grateful.

14. There are no entities in the world. There are only activities.

15. Empty, empty. Happy, happy.

CONTENTS

A SUGGESTION ON HOW TO USE THIS BOOK

This book is a simple collection of stories. Bhante told them and I wrote them in a nonlinear way, meaning, if you start at the beginning you could be starting at the end. We did it like that on purpose, because beginnings and endings are mostly mind-made anyway. Who ever knows when something actually starts or finishes? Grace is hard to measure like that.

Each story has a deliberate brevity — Bhante Sujatha sincerely believes words are limiting and often a distraction from true spiritual practice. "Tyler, please try to include lots of silence in the book!"... an instruction I first found ridiculous and impossible. You'll find I decided to leave some room between each story — a blank page or two for you to write your own story, to contemplate in any way you find worthy. Or perhaps you will preserve the silent emptiness of the page as something equally noble as the words and stories themselves. After all, how could we have the title *Empty, Empty, Happy, Happy* without showing the true beauty of some emptiness?

I hope this becomes a journal for some. I hope others rip it up and make it into an art project. If you are inclined, share. The size and style, I think, have a devotional feel. Hopefully it's portable enough that you can keep it with you and use it as an aid to your meditation practice or as a daily reminder of the simple wisdom that helps our joy rise and our lives deepen.

INTRODUCTION

The temple bell rings. The ring and the reverberation are separate. A hundred-year-old(ish) stained glass depiction of Jesus resides behind us while the ten-foot-tall Buddha statue on the altar greets our attention. Although I can't prove it, I believe (or like to believe) this is the only Buddhist temple in the United States where Jesus and Buddha reside together.

We've become accustomed to rising when the bell rings; the silence enters fast. We used to have someone special light the altar candles, someone who needed blessings or wanted to dedicate the practice. This tradition, however, seems to have faded as we've grown together as a spiritual community. We no longer seem attached to separateness like that.

He smiles. Any thought or plan is eradicated. I become a blank canvas. I become ready.

This is always the case. No use avoiding it anymore. This monk empties me of preconception and helps me choose how to fill back up.

I'm not a tall man, and yet he fits perfectly under my arms when we hug. Our contrast in size leaves me with this feeling of protectiveness for him, a physical reaction. Bhante Sujatha weighs in at 115 pounds. His burgundy monk robes don't add any weight to him, although they bring the same commanding presence and capacity to intimidate as the Pope.

They call him a Buddhist monk. Reverend. Venerable. Holy. The Chief Sangha Nayaka of North America. I stick with calling him my brother, cohort, and noble friend. I had a hard time reconciling our friendship at first. I couldn't accept that I could be this fortunate. Working together running The Blue Lotus Buddhist Temple, studying together, adventuring around the world together in service to others (you'll read more about this at end of the book!) has blown my heart and mind wide open. But none of that lives up to the simple fact of our friendship itself, an unlikely pairing of a Buddhist monk and a white capitalist American. I ask myself often, how did this happen? We don't fit together at all, and yet our friendship is so natural and sturdy and easy and undeniable.

It's a surprise Bhante is here at the Blue Lotus Buddhist Temple and Meditation Center, sixty miles northwest of Chicago in the sleepy little town of Woodstock, Illinois, complete with a cobblestone town square and Saturday farmers' markets, in a historic 1868 former church that Bhante converted to our main temple. Now, however, he's gone what largely feels like all the time. He tells us it's because we don't need him, that the world still needs him. We hate that answer, but we know it's true now. The wisdom he teaches is simple. It doesn't have the depth people think they need. Instead, it's pure. Straightforward. Incomplete. Bhante's teachings make room for us to ponder. He extends an invitation to the deeper well of holiness, but he doesn't go in the well with us or even stick around to make sure we enter. He doesn't want to remind people that he has already offered all there is. He moves on, finding others to invite, leaving us to walk the path alone. Bhante believes that the complex paths we choose and wisdom we study and words we stumble on all lead to the same basic core principles.

People comment occasionally about how the temple's teachings aren't going deep enough. How it can feel repetitive and as if the teachings are only "surface" level practices. Bhante smiles and remains silent amidst these concerns. He believes those who seek deeper wisdom have not yet fully accepted his invitation and have more work to do with the simple teachings he's offered. If we went deeper in an external way, it wouldn't work, he says. The Buddha made it clear: we alone must walk the path. The more we seek more, the more likely it is we've not dwelled in the real, authentic, and straightforward practices that, according to Bhante, hold everything we'll ever need.

The monastics walk to their husk-filled cushions that are slightly elevated from our own. One lights the altar candle, and then we all bow. Bhante invites us to be seated, but a few of us wait. There is a reverence to letting monastics sit first, a code most of us don't follow. When Bhante sits on his cushion, I no longer see my friend. Not even once. He instantly becomes a teacher. Not because of his deep and profound knowledge of the teachings of the Buddha, but because he shares exclusively how he practices the teachings in his daily life. I have never spent time with him and not learned something from his words or actions.

A spotlight shines on our altar and Buddha's face. Time of year dictates how bright the stained-glass Jesus is. The windows have a way of revealing varying beauty at certain times of day. I once counted seventeen shades of blue. When I look around I see the transformation, of the place and within all of us. The neutral color and plainness of everything seems dedicated to the majesty of the stained-glass windows and Buddha's altar. I love these pairings. They feel like our old lives and this life, before a life of practice and after.

Bhante lifts his wooden mallet and strikes his bronze bowl on the side in a way that makes the sound travel all the way to the peak of our temple and back down again, wrapping itself amongst us. Sometimes I'm convinced I can see this sound, and I watch it travel to and from us. The postures we all assume are so familiar now. This is a place of few rules. Chairs. Cushions. Standing. Knees up or down. Erect or not. Bhante requires people to come as they are, and that seems to be a core reason people keep coming back. I notice the freedom more when I visit other places of worship and feel a rigidity and certainty about how things are supposed to go. In many Buddhist environments, rules dictate worship: don't turn your back to the altar, keep your shoes off, shorts must be below the knee, no tank tops, sit like this, stand like this, worship like this. Bhante lets most of that go and invites people to come as they are.

Our eyes are shut long before he asks. We present our silence to him and each other like a gift. Bhante used to guide our meditations, but now he seems to guide us less and less and extend the silence more and more with just an occasional invitation, "Bring your concentration back to your breath...."

The trucks and sounds of commerce outside our temple doors are no match. Many of us tell the story of how convinced we were that we couldn't meditate in a place like this, and yet, we now find those sounds become essential aids to our practice, causing us to find comfort right in the center of the real world.

Thirty minutes come and go. Some days it comes so fast I look around wondering where I am and what happened. Other days each minute stacked on top of the next feels like a burden too heavy to carry. I've finally determined both experiences have the same significance and identical outcome. Somewhere in the middle, Bhante reminds us of the no-rule policy, encouraging us to move and readjust and bring our minds back to our breath.

"Now, mindfully observe your breath and your body, becoming aware of the present moment." Then an awkwardly long pause ensues where some of us begin to pray it's over, fearful he's only at the halfway point. "Make a strong determination to practice meditation at least five or ten minutes every day." That's when we know we've reached the finish line. I'm always so grateful for those words, which have never once come too soon.

"May you be well, happy, and peaceful." That's our cue to bow and prepare for the second part of our practice.

We stretch and recalibrate into the space again. This can feel startling. Sometimes I travel so far away in my thoughts it's a long road back. The lighting is always different than when we began. The stained glass captures the outdoor light, and thirty minutes is just enough time for everything to change. Moments after our eyes open we hear, "Let's do the chants, pages three and four." Pages three and four are found in our newly reprinted devotional books that sit on the top right of our cushions. The chanting was upsetting to me at first, it made me wonder if I had joined a cult. But something about the rhythmic certainty of it and the repetitive nature of doing it every day has a way of settling in. I get it now, the importance of repetition and commitment, that's what allows Dharma to show up in my life when I least expect it and most need it.

After our opening chants, we move to the English translation of the Twin Verses at the beginning of the Dhammapada: "Mind is the forerunner of all states...." Then we read aloud a poem titled "We Believe" that I wrote and always find embarrassing when I hear so many others read it aloud. It expounds on the radical promise and sustaining nature of pure generosity. Then, quietly but always, Bhante says, "Please read out loud 'My Wish'—back of the book." This is the bedrock of our temple, of Bhante's core beliefs and mission. The summary of all we stand for: "May I become at all times, both now and forever, a protector for those without protection, a guide for those who have lost their way, a ship for those with an ocean to cross, a sanctuary for those in danger, a lamp for those without light, a place of refuge for those who lack shelter, and a servant to those in need. By means of these meritorious deeds may I never join with the unwise, only the wise, until the time I obtain Nirvana."

It's only at this point in our practice, already forty minutes in, that Bhante greets us, "Hi everybody, how are you this evening?" We respond in twelve-step meeting style, "Hi, Bhante!" His smile smashes directly into however I'm feeling. I can't help it. Neither can he.

Not until this moment have I ever observed the peculiarity of our greeting each other when we're already halfway through our service. Until we've practiced, nothing else matters. "Put your own oxygen mask on first," Bhante says daily. "You must take care of yourself before you can take care of anyone else. Being self-centered is how you help others!"

Right up until this halfway point greeting, we could be at

almost any Buddhist temple or meditation studio or one of a hundred yoga classes on the upper east side of any big city. Much of what we've done is common. Maybe in your church it's called prayer. I think as a kid we called it quiet time. In yoga, they call it Savasana. There isn't anything that unusual about the chanting. Everyone sings in church, and our version isn't all that different. It's awesome to be in fellowship, what we call our Sangha, but we can meditate anywhere. I have more than ten apps on my iPhone that can lead me in a guided meditation wherever and whenever I want. We all have access to Dharma talks from all the great teachers from all the great traditions now. Wi-Fi has brought the world's wisdom to wherever we are.

But the common, reproducible, and downloadable experience ends right here at this halfway point, right after Bhante says, "Hi, everybody." Bhante looks out at us, at our incomplete and earnest intent, at our desire for more. Sometimes he has a plan, something particular he wants to share. Sometimes I can see him pause and look and wait for the right words. Sometimes he waits for us to ask.

The approach doesn't matter. The words that come are uniquely his brand, his way of presenting Dharma. He knows the Buddha's suttas and other Buddhist teachings. He knows the texts of the Dhammapada. In stark contrast to his robes and this temple and his tradition, he steadfastly commits to not teaching directly and literally from these materials.

Instead, he leans into his craft. His talent that he's built a life around and helped tens of thousands of people with. Bhante is a storyteller. He takes wisdom and essential core teachings and turns them into story. Stories of how things work in the real world, how wisdom can be applied. He introduces concepts and action plans. He demonstrates how love is a verb and how important words can be, what it actually takes to dedicate your life to serving others. He models for us, through his intentionally conscious daily actions, how to live with nobility and add more love. He turns wisdom and Dharma into tools we can pick up and use ourselves to make our lives and the world better.

We're celebrating our first fifteen years here at the Blue Lotus Temple and Bhante's fiftieth birthday. In all that time, Bhante hasn't run out of stories, so you'd think retelling them here would take volumes. But it won't. Bhante believes people seek a spiritual life in only two ways:

> 1. By searching far and wide, bolstering their intellect, reading volumes and studying all great wisdom. This is something he calls Head Dharma.
>
> 2. By going deep and narrow, taking a few core principles and concepts and really working them to the bone. Truly integrating them into daily life, directly to the heart of your actions. This is what he calls Heart Dharma.

Bhante will meet you wherever you are. If it's far and wide, he'll go along with you. But if it's deep and narrow, he's ready to dive. It's the second he prefers. "A few simple practices, repeated and practiced over and over for a lifetime, that is all you need," Bhante says.

This simple monk wants you to do, not say. To feel, not just to know. "I want you to know and feel a few simple teachings and use them every single day to make your life and our world better." Otherwise, he asks, "What's the point?"

In preparation for writing this book, I didn't have to spend much direct time with Bhante to recount these stories. Knowing him and living deep in our friendship and this spiritual practice has given me the great benefit of hearing all these stories firsthand. I was surprised to learn I could retell them with ease. We have attended thousands of meditations together. We have traveled the world and sat in airports, delayed and tired and talking for hours. We have hiked pilgrim trails and suburban sidewalks for hours and days discussing and contemplating what his basic core principles really are, what mine are, and what the teachings of the Buddha tells us. Over the years, I've asked so many questions, some over and over again, and Bhante has never got tired of answering. "What do you really stand for? What matters most to you? Why do you believe that? Tell me more. Tell me more. Tell me more." I'd ask, and then he'd talk, and I'd take mental notes that eventually turned into all this. I hope you will come to know Bhante by reading these simple stories. I know him from living this life with him directly— we work together, he leads our spiritual community, and I serve him as President of Temple, doing whatever I can to help make it all run well. I see him on good and bad days, and he sees me the same. Somehow, we've accepted each other entirely, shortcomings and all.

Bhante taught me that we seek wisdom in three ways: thinking, listening, and meditating. I try to listen whenever I'm around him. Turns out he listens to me, too. I see how he has learned to navigate American life and better relate to all of us as a result. It's not an equal exchange, and I feel profoundly indebted, but I have also stopped measuring and have learned a core Bhante teaching: accept the blessings that show up.

This book is my attempt to repay Bhante and to share his gift with the world, his absolute core essential teachings, told through story. Teachings that we can dwell within, work on, live with, and have. They are written in first person, something I spent considerable time contemplating. Bhante's English is broken and cherished by his students, although it's not always understandable at first take. I eventually decided on writing in cleaned-up but not perfect English, so that any reader can feel him and still understand the story. I set out to represent what happens in the second half of our daily practices at the Blue Lotus Buddhist Temple. These stories are the Dharma talks you can't duplicate, the juicy pearls of pure grace and wisdom that only Bhante Sujatha can share. I have done my best to write and retell these stories, to have you experience the magic of his words and his smile through this limited word-bound format. It's flawed and incomplete, that is for sure. However, the essential wisdom of Bhante Sujatha resides within these stories, and the peace and happiness we all seek awaits.

My hope, and Bhante's, is for these stories to aid us all in our practice and commitment to be well, happy, and peaceful.

Tyler Lewke

Woodstock, IL, USA

May, 2017

WHAT IS A BHANTE SUJATHA?

When Bhante Sujatha was ten years old, he told his parents he would throw himself off the bridge into the river that ran near his childhood home in Peradeniya, Sri Lanka, if they did not let him become a monk. For the next forty years he's remained that certain and determined to live a life dedicated to adding more love to the world and helping people heal their wounded minds. Born in 1967, Bhante was the younger of two children and the only son, making his parents' approval of his calling harder to get in a culture where the son grows up to take care of the family. When they finally granted him permission to ordain, Bhante entered the Subodharama International Monk Training Center, a now-famous training school. This temple is a part of the Theravada tradition of Buddhism. Theravada is regarded among its practitioners as the lineage closest to the original form of Buddhism. It was brought to Sri Lanka (formerly Ceylon) in 250 BCE and is now widespread through many other Southeast Asian countries including India, Thailand, Burma, Laos, and Kampuchea (Cambodia). As a novice monk, Bhante trained under the school's ordination teacher, the Venerable Dhammawasa Thero.

Bhante has always known he was born to serve humanity and

he wakes up every day committed to the noble cause of teaching meditation and helping people access the deeper parts of themselves so they can feel radiant joy and peaceful happiness. Even at his young age of ordination, he eagerly adhered to the strict trainings of monastic life.

Compared to that of their American counterparts, the life young boys in Buddhist monasteries is rigid. At Subodharama, young monks were expected to rise at 4:00 a.m. and make tea for all the other members of the temple before beginning their chanting and meditation practice at 5:00 a.m. Only two meals a day were served at the temple—breakfast and a large lunch. After breakfast, the boys studied the Buddhist scriptures, followed by more chanting and study time. At 11:00 a.m., they showered and laundered their robes. Lunch was followed by five hours of study in the classroom, and at 5:00 p.m. it was time for a second round of temple cleaning. This was followed by more meditation and chanting, and then another round of study time. Bedtime for the young monks came at 9:30 or 10:00 p.m.

Following his graduation, Bhante served as a teacher at Subodharama for two years. Then in 1993, with one set of robes and enough food wrapped up for the first leg of his journey, Bhante left his home country for Brisbane, Australia, where he taught meditation and Buddhism at the Sri Lankaramaya Buddhist Monastery. Four years later, he was asked by one of his former Subodharama teachers, the Venerable Mudtha Thero, to join him in the United States. He found his way to America where he continued learning the English language and culture and recognized the aching desire people have for a more meaningful life. He relocated to the midwestern United States from Australia and helped found the Great Lakes Buddhist

Vihara in Southfield, Michigan. Five years later, after obtaining his permanent residency in the United States, Bhante decided it was time to do something different. Although he enjoyed spending time with the Sri Lankan community in the Michigan, he wanted to help his fellow Americans, who always seemed "vaguely dissatisfied despite their many possessions and high standard of living" and seemed to be "constantly striving after the next best thing."

Bhante began sending out exploratory emails and got in touch with several Unitarian churches across the United States. He started communicating with the Congregational Unitarian Church of Woodstock, Illinois, who invited him to visit. When he came to visit, Bhante toured McHenry County College and said he felt "really good and happy" there. He decided Woodstock was a good place for him to be and again left all he knew for a new adventure. "I always follow my heart," says Bhante.

After enrolling as a student at McHenry to better learn English and pursue a degree in psychology, he was approached by Reverend Dan Larsen of the Unitarian Church in Woodstock about starting a meditation class. Bhante agreed, and in January of 2003 he began teaching meditation in an old leaky church basement. The first night, two people showed up. Fifteen years later, The Blue Lotus Buddhist Temple and Meditation Center has become a well-known temple that serves thousands of people locally and even more around the world under Bhante's leadership as the abbot and spiritual director.

Fifth-graders often tower over Bhante, but make no mistake, this man is a powerhouse of focus, energy, and determination. Each year, Bhante leads more than 380 meditations and travels hundreds of thousands of miles, often walking off a plane and onto a podium within minutes of arriving at his destination. He speaks to colleges and universities across the world, leads small group retreats, and consults with corporate giants, teaching them all that love is the way and peace is a constant practice. Bhante's humanitarian work spans the globe. Recently he oversaw the retrofitting of several rural hospitals in Sri Lanka using donated medical equipment from America worth millions of dollars.

Bhante believes his job here in America is not only teaching meditation but also "teaching people how to be happy." His primary goal is to help people apply the teachings of the Buddha to their everyday lives. According to Bhante, "The core essence of all the Buddha's teachings is the same, but how things are done and the ways people are guided are different." He explains, "We can get into the ocean in different ways, or from different places, but it's still the same ocean."

Bhante Sujatha says that he "believes in change rather than tradition," particularly when dealing with life in our fast-paced Western society. His approach to teaching is easygoing rather than dogmatic, and he makes every attempt to explain things to his American audience so that even absolute beginners can understand how to practice meditation and how to apply the spiritual teachings to their own daily lives. "I help people here by teaching them to see their jobs and work as a form of spiritual practice," he says. "Then they can learn to enjoy whatever they are doing in the moment, instead of always worrying about the future or the past. That's the most important thing."

For monks, Bhante further explains, "meditation is a very different practice than for regular people living in a community." Since monks spend most of their time in a cloistered environment away from the rest of society, they do not face many of the same challenges as other people who must contend with family and relationship stresses, along with the intense pressures that career and daily life often entail. Fortunately for Westerners, Bhante maintains that daily life can become an excellent form of meditation, if you can learn to view your whole life as a form of spiritual practice. In this way, whenever we are faced with difficult situations in our daily lives, we learn to retrain our minds and become "mindful" of our feelings and emotions, and learn to practice kindness, compassion, and patience instead of anger, vengefulness, and intolerance. In this way, not only do we become more peaceful ourselves, but we also become more positive influences on the world around us.

As a spiritual leader and teacher, Bhante believes his job is to "prepare the field for other people, who—when they achieve happiness—will hopefully plant the seeds and do the rest." In 2013, Bhante Sujatha was awarded the highest honor within his sect as a recognition for the incredible impact he's made spreading the Buddha's teachings across America and was named the Chief Sangha Nayaka of North America.

On any given day, you'll find Bhante on the West Coast leading retreats, in the Midwest running the temple and inspiring people to give and do even more to help the world, or on the other side of the planet providing refuge for those who suffer. This man is literally tireless, often sleeping three or four hours a night and using every single waking moment with total purpose and dedication to his mission: adding more love to the world.

ABOUT BUDDHISM

Technically speaking, Buddhism is a set of wisdom teachings we call the Dharma that encompasses a wide variety of traditions and spiritual practices based on the original oral teachings of the Buddha who lived in India 2,600ish years ago. Some call it a religion. Some call it a philosophy. More on this later. For now, I'm not going to write a description of the life of the Buddha or how Buddhism was formed. You can Google a thousand references to that stuff. Instead I'm going to give you my flawed and imperfect answer to this unanswerable question: what is Buddhism, really? To even pose this question invites disharmony and immediate scrutiny (and some inevitable eye rolling). But who cares? To understand Buddhism is to understand that disharmony is always present, scrutiny is always present, and that someone, in fact, many people, will always roll their eyes at you. Maybe I could describe Buddhism as the tools to manage disharmony and scrutiny, both from the world and from the wounded parts of ourselves where we self-loathe and sabotage our own opportunity for inner peace.

If I posed the question to a broad audience, a bunch of folks would say Buddhism is a religion. An equal or greater number would say it's not a religion. Many would say Buddhism can pair with other religions perfectly, for example, I know groups of people who call themselves "Christian Buddhists" and "Muslim Buddhists" and "Jewish Buddhists." A great number of folks refer to themselves as "atheist Buddhists." I won't make an argument one way or the other on any of these labels, but I will offer some supporting evidence.

> Jesus: "Love your enemies, do good to those who hate you, bless those who curse you, pray for those who abuse you. From anyone who takes away your coat do not withhold even your shirt. Give to everyone who begs from you; and if anyone takes away your goods, do not ask for them again." (Luke 6.27–30)

> Buddha: "Hatreds do not ever cease in this world by hating, but by love; this is an eternal truth...Overcome anger by love, overcome evil by good. Overcome the miser by giving, overcome the liar by truth." (Dhammapada 1.5 &17.3)

> Muhammed: "Kindness is a mark of faith, and whoever is not kind has no faith."Jesus: "How hard it will be for those who have wealth to enter the kingdom of God! It is easier for a camel to go through the eye of a needle than for someone who is rich to enter the kingdom of God." (Mark 10.23 & 25)

> Buddha: "Riches make most people greedy, and so are like caravans lurching down the road to perdition. Any

possession that increases the sin of selfishness or does nothing to confirm one's wish to renounce what one has is nothing but a drawback in disguise." (Jatakamala 5.5 & 15)

Muhammed: "The best richness is the richness of the soul." (Book 005: Hadith 2287)

Frankly, to fully answer the question, "What is Buddhism?" would be to violate one of the core teachings of the Buddha, "Come and see, don't come and believe," so I won't do that. Instead, here is a simple perspective Bhante Sujatha and I share.

The Buddha gave instruction on how to navigate this life. Buddha's teachings have nothing at all to do with religion. Buddhism has rituals and dogma and a belief system — "Buddha did not make Buddhism, people did," says Bhante. Buddhism is religion, and people invented Buddhism and all the other "isms," but Buddhisms is not synonymous with the Buddha's teachings. Buddha's teachings gave us tools and instruction for how to handle the difficulties of life and the suffering that arises. "He taught us how to handle things," Bhante Sujatha often says. The core of Buddha's teachings is very specific: the Four Noble Truths and the Eightfold Path. "That's it. There is nothing else," Bhante says. Any time an "ism" is attached to a set of teachings, it creates problems in the world, and the teachings become limited. They create divisions and fractions and work to separate us rather than unite us. Religion is fear-based, the teachings of The Buddha are mindfulness-based.

I like to consider the Four Noble Truths as something for us

to understand, and the Noble Eightfold Path as something for us
do. Understanding leads to action which leads to liberation.

THE FOUR NOBLE TRUTHS

The Four Noble Truths are the foundation of Buddha's
teachings.

> 1. The truth that being alive means we will experience
> suffering.

> 2. The truth of the cause of that suffering.

> 3. The truth that the end of our suffering experience
> is possible.

> 4. The truth that a clear eightfold path, when
> practiced, leads to the end of suffering.

"Suffering exists, it has a cause, it has an end, it has a cause
to bring about its end," says Bhante Sujatha. Some feel aversion
to Buddha's teaching because he used this word "suffering" often
and people don't like it. "But we do suffer. We deal with our
bodies getting old, people dying, loss, mental instability, desire,
ignorance, craving," says Bhante Sujatha. "The Buddha gave us
clear tools to alleviate the suffering these experiences bring."

THE EIGHTFOLD PATH

(also often referred to as "The Middle Path" or "The Middle Way")

The Eightfold Path is considered the heart of the Buddhist

teachings. Probably every religion uses some different words but has a nearly identical intention. The Eightfold Path is made up of Right View, Right Intention, Right Action, Right Speech, Right Livelihood, Right Effort, Right Mindfulness, and Right Concentration. It's simple enough to understand—our views and intentions and actions and speech and how we earn money and the effort we put forth and the mindfulness and concentration we put into things is more than enough to work on, and if we just make sure we're noble in these eight areas, we will probably have an amazing life.

The Eightfold Path is commonly called "the Path" and is considered a road map for us to explore, test, and practice as a way to live every day with nobility. In following and practicing the path, you learn to see life as it is, to accept it and embrace it and find the joy in any circumstance.

1. **RIGHT VIEW**: Be aware of your own actions and the reasons behind them. Know the Four Noble Truths and see the world as it really is, drop the illusions. Remember everything (even us!) changes and that clinging to the idea of that it (or we) won't is an illusion and gives rise to unhappiness. When we stop expecting things to always be good and start embracing reality, life gets so much better.

2. **RIGHT INTENTION**: Understand what controls you, how you make decisions. Are your choices for the good of all or just yourself? Resist acting on feelings of desire,

prejudgment, or aggression. Pause and reflect, then act. This will save you from a world of hurt. Inquire why you are doing what you're doing. Knowing why is so helpful.

3. **RIGHT SPEECH**: Words are weapons and peace makers. Words make and break our lives. When we speak in judgment of others, gossip, or spread untrue statements, we are participating in the causes of suffering. We must be extreme in our carefulness with the things we say. Don't tell deliberate lies or speak deceitfully. Avoid using harsh words that offend or hurt others. Speak kindly and only if you have something positive to contribute. "Noble silence is a great protector of the heart," Bhante says.

4. **RIGHT ACTION**: Be in service to others. Help where you can. Don't harm, don't kill, don't steal, don't sexually misuse anyone. Do good works. Simple, not easy. Be your brothers' and sisters' keeper.

5. **RIGHT LIVELIHOOD**: Be conscious of the work you choose. Live honestly, find ways to have your work benefit mankind. Avoid occupations that violate your commitment to the Path, especially right speech and right action.

6. **RIGHT EFFORT**: Just do it. Effort is the foundation of all of the other Eightfold Path steps. Without right effort, you can't get anywhere really. You make no

progress on your path to inner peace. We have to work hard, tell the truth, and love the people. Actively engage in the world around you and help others to help yourself. Put in the time for service, study, and spiritual practice.

7. **RIGHT MINDFULNESS**: "Be here now" is a simple statement but not easy to practice. We live vast amounts of time in the past or the future. Pausing and learning to look at yourself from a distance is the foundation of mindfulness. A simple pause, an overview of how you are feeling, an observation of how you're feeling in your body and in your mind. Notice what's happening, stay in inquiry to why you are feeling what you are feeling. Seek the source. Don't judge or interpret these observations, just observe them. The eighth step of the Path is how you achieve this mindfulness.

8. **RIGHT CONCENTRATION**: Meditation builds up good habits. Our behavior changes gradually. Our anger decreases, we are more able to make thoughtful and wise decisions. We become more satisfied and restful. We can love more fully, ourselves and all others, and through a strong determination to practice meditation, our lives reach a state of harmony not otherwise obtainable.

Deeply knowing the Four Noble Truths and following and practicing the Eightfold Path helped my judgments fall away and has given me motivation and strength to up my kindness in all my affairs, to be more aware and thoughtful in every exchange, to empty my mind and drop the mental noise and anguish that can torment me. The delusions that I manufacture seem to dissipate and even when they still show up, I catch them sooner. I'm more able to recognize what's happening and get back to center more quickly.

Buddhist scripture says the Eightfold Path leads to liberation from our suffering and to an awakened, enlightened life. I don't know about those things. What I do know is that when I practice these principles in all my affairs, my life becomes easier, full of joy and peace, and suffused with sustainable happiness. Is it like that all the time? Of course not. Some days still totally suck. But with a rigorous commitment to keep at it, I find myself coming back to center faster and faster—and I stay on a little longer each time.

Every day, I remind myself of the Eightfold Path in one way or another. I read and study ancient teachings about the steps, and I listen to how others use them to navigate their lives. Mostly, I set my intentions to live in nobility and kindness, to follow this path wherever my life goes. I do this not because some scripture says to or because of any religious instruction. I do it because I see the evidence. I see fruitage show up all over the lives of people who walk this ancient road. "The teachings of Buddha reveal a step-by-step path to lasting happiness," says Bhante Sujatha.

TYING THE CAT

Story 1

Hi, everybody, how are you this evening?

"Hi, Bhante!"

Tonight is one of those nights that if I was still in my home country of Sri Lanka, I would get in big trouble! I was trained in traditional Buddhism at the Subodharama International Monk Training Center. I lived in a traditional village and had strict instruction on how to study the teachings of the Buddha and how to share the Dharma with people. We practiced many, many days on what to say and how to say it to all the people. What is on my mind tonight to share with you is not something I ever would talk about in those formal settings, but I feel it on my heart, so I want to share because I feel people so confused. Even I am confused sometimes.

We live in a marketing culture where things get packed and sold to us, even beliefs. I am always worrying what is real and what is just believed to be real because someone made it seem so. This is really good lesson, something for you to always be looking out for: what is the truth?

I believe Buddha's teaching doesn't have a shape. It is shapeless, formless. It's not organized the way other teachings are. It's often oral, casual, passed down from one to another. We call it Buddhist Dharma or Buddhist practice. I like the word practice best. Before I was a monk, my mother would often curl up next to the coconut husk-filled pad I slept on and tell me stories of the Buddha's time. Our tiny home, with mud walls and a dirt floor, was where I first understood who the Buddha was and what his life represented. Even now, when I recently went to visit my mom and dad, they were watching a television program of the Buddha's life. I guess this is the modern way of sharing the stories. Who knows what the future of delivering the Dharma to people will be?

Now, 2,600 years after the Buddha, I can see Buddhism is starting to have a shape. It has one big shape itself, and then there are so many other shapes surrounding it. Buddhism is a big shape. Then we have Indian Buddhists and Korean Buddhists and Japanese Buddhists and Sri Lankan Buddhists. These smaller shapes all come from the bigger shape. Now people are so worrying about those smaller shapes. They are ranking them good, bad, right, wrong.

My analogy is, Buddhism is like water in a container. Water does not have a shape, right? Water takes the shape of anything you put it in. Maybe we call it a glass of water or a bottle of water. Buddha's teachings do not have a shape themselves, but like water, we pour Buddhism into our own glass or bottle. The glass being our cultures and the bottle being our traditions. So many people, myself included, are living in these shapes and believing their shape is great, right, real. We begin to believe our way is the truth.

But it is not. People are worrying about the container more than the content. If someone touches my container, or I move my container even one inch in a different direction, people get mad. Why? Because we're all so attached to our containers, to our cultures and traditions. We believe our culture and tradition is Buddhism. We forget to drink to quench our thirst, and instead we drink because others before us have done so.

We become our own slaves. We begin to believe what we created instead of what the Buddha taught. We have to practice the teachings and work to let go of the container. I struggle with this every day, but I remain committed because it is so important. A core teaching of the Buddha is that everything changes, it is always changing. So, we have to be vigilant in looking out for things we do just because we always did. I believe a great use of our time is to measure what is serving us now and what is no longer serving us, even if it did before. Things come in seasons, you know? Like so many flowers bloom in spring but not winter. We had the most beautiful meadow in Sri Lanka. I will never forget how beautiful it was. I would walk the long windy path from my house to the meadow, and as the seasons changed, all the wild flowers changed. One flower I fell so in love with and I would always pick it and bring it to my mom. I loved seeing her smile spread and fill her whole face. A mom's job in my village is really hard, and even as young boy, I knew my job was to help her smile. I spent the whole season every day going to get that smile flower. Then it was gone. The season changed. I waited a whole year for the season to come back that brought the smile flower, but it never came. Only one season, in one year, did that flower come. I am a fifty-year-old monk now, and I still go search for that one flower, but it is still not there. Do you know what happened? I never again brought my mom a flower. I felt without that one special smile flower, no other flowers were good. I missed all that beauty, and I missed my mom's smile, because I became so attached to that one thing. This experience has been a big influence in my life. I think we all get obsessed with one flower and miss the field of flowers.

I want to tell you a story to explain. There was a temple with a very famous monk who used to live there. Every evening, the monk and the students were practicing their evening meditation. The bell rang, and everyone came to the meditation hall. Right after they sat to practice, the temple cat came to the meditation hall and was distracting everyone—it was meowing, annoying to all the yogis. The cat was annoying to the monk, also.

One day the monk said, "The cat is making all this noise and bothering our meditation. Please tie up this cat to the porch outside when the meditation bell rings."

Every day the meditation bell would ring, and the young students would tie up the cat on the porch before beginning practice. This became a big tradition at this temple. Eventually the cat passed away. Without tying up the cat, none of the practitioners could meditate. The monk said, "Go and get a new cat, and tie him up!"

Many years and cats and monks later, an entirely new generation of monks and students live at the temple. They have no idea why they have a cat they tie up to the porch before meditation, but they always do it. Maybe more than one hundred cats' lifetimes, and it is still happening today. All the monks there believe they cannot meditate in that place without a cat tied up.

We all do this in small ways. We believe in conditions and containers. When we work to free ourselves and go to the true teachings of the Buddha, we find a peace and ease that I have come to rely upon.

Ok, everybody, thank you very much and have a good night. Please, let's bow together now, ok?

"Thank you, Bhante."

CONTEMPLATIONS

---

*We must learn to live in truth,
as it always outlasts falsehood.*

CONTEMPLATIONS

YOU ARE A TERRIBLE BUDDHIST MONK!

—

Story 2

Hi, everybody, how are you this evening?

"Hi, Bhante!"

I've been thinking about my first few years in this country. I think I've been here in America more than twenty years now, I lose track. Oh my, if you knew me then you would laugh so hard at how I got around and figured things out. I made so many mistakes, ordering wrong food, going wrong direction on roads. I remember the first escalator I ever stood on, I could not believe my eyes that stairs moved!

I was so confused by people and this culture. I quickly realized I couldn't tell how people were actually doing versus what they were just saying to me. I couldn't read their heart the way I could in my country because even that required translation from one culture to another. As a solution, I decided to do personal interviews with people who were coming to meditation. I hoped to eventually gain the skill to understand how people were feeling, not just what they were saying. In my country, there is not much difference, but here in America, I learned it's a big difference!

Over and over again, by the end of the personal interview, the people were crying and seemingly full of self-hatred and anger. I found many people so emotional and unhappy. I made a name for the pain I saw; I called it their "wounded mind." I realized how many people suffered from a wounded mind, and right away I realized helping to heal the wounded mind would become a big part of my monking job in this country.

My first meditations taught me so much. I was so scared, shaking like a leaf in the wind! But people were so kind to me. I had little index cards I wrote my notes on, so I would remember English words. Sometimes my hands shook so much I couldn't read the cards. I am grateful for that experience, it taught me the value of hard work and preparation, and that fear is something to notice but not let stop me. As a group they showed up always smiling and happy, but individually I found they were so unhappy. I realized they smiled in the group but were miserable privately. I felt that their happiness existed somewhere in them, so hope and healing was possible. It inspired me. I became committed to practicing self-love with them and helping them become authentically happy.

The first time I taught loving-kindness meditation, I asked everyone to focus their practice towards themselves instead of others. Many people get good at loving others, but loving ourselves is a much harder task. After those first few meditations I asked for feedback, and unanimously they agreed it was a lot of work, and loving others was so much easier than loving ourselves.

After one meditation, a woman with an angry face came to see me. She was very upset. She said she hated loving-kindness practice. It didn't make any sense to her, and she explained she could easily understand loving other people, but she couldn't understand how or why to love herself. She said this is not her culture, not her religion, and that it was self-centered, the opposite of what she thought we should be working on.

I suggested to her, "You cannot practice loving-kindness without starting with yourself."

She disagreed. She explained she helped the homeless every week, and she did lots of other things to help people. She felt like any attention on herself was selfish. I understood her feelings. I asked, "If you don't have self-love, how can you give it to others?" She was so quiet. I continued, "If you give me a gift, after the gift what do you expect to hear from me?" She answered, "I want to hear you say thank you." I replied, "And if I don't say it?" "Then you are a terrible Buddhist monk," she said, joking but not totally joking. My first year in this country I realized when people joke, some kernel of truth always lives in the joke. I am very careful about this.

I was quiet a moment before responding to her. "After you give me a gift, my practice and responsibility is to say thank you and appreciate you. That is my job as a human being. But if you have an expectation for my thank you, then that is your problem, you have to handle that. Waiting for my 'thank you' makes the gift about you feeling good, but the gift was supposed to be for me."

She didn't like what I said at all. Without another word, she grabbed her purse and left. I worried I messed up my English words like I have done many times. Once I commented on a woman's weight and she was devastated. In our country, the bigger you are, the more food your village has and the more successful your family life is. Skinny in my country means you are poor and unhealthy and struggling. I just didn't know any better. Now I always ask people to listen to my heart first and my words second. My heart is pure, my words not as much, you understand?

Later that night I got a long email from her: "You hurt my feelings. I don't like the group anymore. I won't be back."

I responded, "I understand how you feel, but still I feel you must learn to love yourself before you can help others, and I want to help."

"No," she responded. "I don't agree with you."

She continued to argue with me, and for weeks I received many negative emails and ugly words. Eventually, I felt she was just pushing my buttons. Loving-kindness is not foolishness. I wrote her to say I would no longer be opening her emails and wished her well. I got many additional emails, but I deleted them without reading them.

After a few months, I got another email. The subject said: "Be kind. Please read." As I read her words, I began to cry. Her email was a perfect example of why I say we all have wounded minds. "Bhante, today is my fortieth birthday, and I can't carry this anger and hatred anymore. I want to surrender. I cannot love myself. I am so angry with my mother and all the people who've hurt me. When I was ten years old, I used to live with my mom, a single, drug-addicted woman who emotionally and physically abused me. I've hated her for that. For so many years, I didn't have any connection with her at all. Today, I woke up and realized I don't want to die carrying this anger for the rest of my life."

I was so happy to read her words. I saw the real blessings of loving-kindness and just how powerful it can be. When she learned to love herself, she found even more love for others. This is what loving-kindness can do.

"I felt a release, a kindness and love towards myself and my mother. I realized, if my mom had known better, she never would have done this to me," she continued.

I responded with a kind email to her, but I did not invite her back. I felt it was her job to come back on her terms when she was ready.

A few months later, while I was getting ready for meditation, I saw an older woman trying to come in through the handicap access. I didn't know her, but I felt I needed to support and help, so I walked towards her. When I got close, I noticed someone coming up behind her. I recognized right away it was the woman bringing her mother to meditation.

Seeing the healing of that mother and daughter was so beautiful to me. This is enough for me, proof that by healing our wounded minds and loving ourselves, we can heal the whole world. We must put our own oxygen mask on first. We all read so many books and watch movies and talk about helping make the world peaceful, helping people feel better, helping the sick and the dying and the needy. This is all wonderful, but no way out but in. We must help ourselves to help the world. If we want the world to be peaceful, we have to learn peace in us. If we want to love the world, we must see that we are the world, too, and learn to love ourselves.

You don't have to do all at once. Just try little bit each day. Wake up, put your feet on ground, and thank your feet for holding you up all day. Let your love start small, in your feet! Love your feet, then soon you will love your whole self. You understand?

When you do this, soon you will be able to find enough love in you for all of you and all of whole world. Practicing loving-kindness meditation, over and over again, even just five minutes a day, you will find love for yourself rise and this will change whole world. Please do it. I will keep doing, too. Together, we will change everything!

Ok, everybody, thank you very much and have a good night. Please, let's bow together now, ok?

"Thank you, Bhante."

CONTEMPLATIONS

---

*Words without actions are just
empty sounds.*

BOOMERANG KARMA

—

Story 3

Hi, everybody, how are you this evening?

"Hi, Bhante!"

Tonight, instead of thinking about what I want to talk about, I am consumed with thinking about what I don't want to talk about. I don't want to talk about next-life Karma. You want to, I know because you always ask me, but I see how this makes a mess of your life. Laypeople and monks alike often describe Karma as: "What we do now will affect our next lives." Or people blame the mess of their life today on Karma from a past life. This thinking makes an even bigger mess. This thinking requires you to understand and believe in next life or past life. I find most people either avoid the subject or misuse the language around it, using it as a rationale for their life situation.

Tonight, I want to clear all this up. I don't need you to believe anything about next or past life, because I can prove what you do today matters right now, in this next hour, next day, not just in your next life. If you cast an uneducated vote today, what happens tomorrow? If you don't sleep tonight, what happens tomorrow? If you say something mean to your partner today, what happens right away? Big mess, right? Lots of suffering. Same goes for the beautiful things in life, too. If you plant a flower bulb today, it blooms in a few months, right? This is a helpful way to think about Karma.

During his life, the Buddha gave monks ten things to reflect on. The eighth was Karma. He said, "Of Karma I am constituted. Karma is my inheritance, Karma is my origin, Karma is my kinsman, Karma is my refuge. Whatever Karma I perform, be it good or bad, to that I shall be heir."

I love these words from the Buddha, but people misunderstand them. The inheritance Buddha talks about is right now. You get your inheritance right away. Karma is not something that we need to believe happens as a result of a past life. We don't need to believe in Karma at all. I know I am a Buddhist monk, and I know what all the other teachers say about Karma, but it is not working. We are still messing up our lives, so I think we don't yet get it, I think I have done a bad job teaching about it. I want to try again.

Understanding Karma can be this simple. For every action there is a reaction. I call it Boomerang Karma, you know, boomerang? You throw, and right away it comes back to you. Cause equals effect, you understand?

To receive happiness and love and peace and friendship, you must be happy. You must be peaceful and loving and a noble friend. Right now. Not another time or another life, do it now!

Just forget about all our fancy Buddhist words. They are worthless if not understood sincerely. Focus all your intention on right now, right in this present moment. Be kind now. Be compassionate right now. Be as mindful as you can be as often as you can be. Living and practicing like this, you will never have to worry about karma. Stop thinking your actions will show in another lifetime, they will show up this afternoon! They will knock you on your butt, right away! Or, they will lift you higher, to a more joyful and peaceful life.

When I was a kid, we learned a lot about Karma. Karma is a Sanskrit word meaning action. My teacher taught me Karma is not for punishment, but it can feel like that sometimes. Right away if we do something bad, something bad happens, right?

What's important to know is, we only suffer if we have created conditions for suffering. Our mind is our most powerful weapon. We create the world we live in, all of us together. Imagine our world if more people knew this.

There are what some call "laws" of Karma that I want to invite you to consider because I think this makes it simple to practice and understand. If we don't understand, what's the point, right? Let's call this a practice in Right Understanding:

1. **CAUSE AND EFFECT**: Our actions have consequences, both good and bad. Sometimes right away, sometimes delayed, right? Our lives would be forever changed if we just remembered this and acted accordingly. We must create the world we desire.

2. **CREATION**: It's our job. We must put forth the effort of good things for good things to happen. Our intentions are mostly what our Karma is judged upon.

When I was a boy, and walked the cow down to the river, my intention was good, to do my job and help my family. If something bad happened to the cow as we walked, no bad Karma came to me. We must participate in goodness so goodness comes to us. We must participate in the bad thing to be responsible for it.

3. **HUMILITY**: This is a big job. Maybe our only job in this lifetime. Above all we can do and practice, if we just work on humility, everything else will come. For me, bowing is the greatest form of humility and surrender. Being humble means we accept life as it shows up. When we refuse to accept what is, Karma will get us. When we accept what is, we suffer less and have the energy to help make a difference. When you truly practice humility, it's hard to have bad Karma show up. Focus on what we want, and we'll get it. Focus on what's wrong, and it grows.

4. **GROWTH**: To grow, we must change. Right? We all know this. Our kids grow and what happens? They get bigger and smarter, and their whole bodies change. Same for our insides and our spiritual life. We must put our growth and practice above all else. When we do, Karma will support us. The effort of your practice will show up when you least expect, right when you need it most. It's hard to always be working on yourself, but you must do it. Make a strong determination. It will be like the boomerang, and the good merits come right back to you.

5. **RESPONSIBILITY**: We are responsible for our life. Suffering is created by us, by how we look at things. If something bad is happening in the world, it's our job to help make things better. We can't help the whole world, but we can help our own world. I feel this all time when I travel, a responsibility to help show people how to find peace inside. I do my best. No bad Karma comes to me when I own my responsibility as a monk. When I see suffering and I don't help, I suffer and create a future legacy of suffering.

6. **CONNECTION**: When a butterfly flaps his wings in another country, it can be felt in small ways around the whole world. Both small and large actions are connected, and sometimes we can't even see results until we are looking in life's rearview mirror, you understand? If we want something to change, often we must look at what it's connected to a long time ago. We have to get to the root. My body is sick all the time, you know? I have to look at what I eat, how I sleep, what I did a long time ago not to take good care. Maybe this life or past, I don't know, it doesn't matter, I'm still sick. Our past and today and tomorrow are all connected, so we must pay attention, even when we aren't sure why. Our actions matter and will bring good or bad results right now and down the road. This is Karma.

7. **FOCUS**: To get what we want, sometimes we have to let other stuff crash. People think we can do multiple

things at once. I think that's not right. To really go deep and change our insides, we have to direct all our attention. Sometimes this can look messy. When I built The Blue Lotus Temple, I didn't do lots of other things, I neglected myself and my time, and I didn't pay close attention to some friends and family. I poured all my energy into this single goal for a period of time. I may have some Karma to deal with, a cost of the extreme focus. I think this is okay, like credit and debit in my checking account. My intention wasn't to cause trouble, but my focus was all-consuming. In pursuit of spiritual practices, this sometimes happens. I think it's worth it.

8. **GIVING**: In the book *A Course in Miracles*, they have a saying, "To have, give all to all." I believe they got this right. Giving can be a very selfish thing—to get goodness we must give it. To receive love, we must first learn how to give it. To have money, we must learn generosity. I think the spiritual life is impossible without it. We read "We Believe" at the temple at every practice. This poem talks about extreme generosity and how generosity is what saves us and makes life possible. Giving requires mindfulness and pure intention, we can give with a generous heart, or we can give for ego, for self-gratification. The receiver gets what you offer, but your Karma will be different depending on your motivation. Watch carefully. It's better to give less and give authentically with pure motivation than to give a

lot and not have good intent. The second will catch up to you. The first will sustain you.

9. **CHANGE:** I think today can change yesterday. I know this is confusing, let me explain. If something bad happens and you learn from it, you have changed history. You made the past different. You stopped the cycle. You've made the bad thing good. What you perceived as bad, once you've gotten the lesson of it, you look back and see it as good. As a result, change is always happening. How we react to change creates Karma. Think about it, if something bad is happening and you blow up in anger, not only is your past suffering, but now your future will, too, because the anger comes right back to you. Boomerang. Learning to pause, to sit in non-reaction, to grab hold of your mindfulness in these critical moments, this is so important. You learn this, and you'll have the ability to impact your whole life. History repeats itself unless we change the cycle.

10. **BE HERE NOW:** Have you walked down the street and bumped into someone or something because you were on your phone? Yes? Me, too! So many times. This is such a great example of our problem. We have become addicted to not being where we are. We use our devices as companionship and distraction. To get us away from this moment. If this moment is so bad or boring, we need to work on it, but our distractions hide that reality

most of the time. When we are present, our future Karma will be directly impacted. It's harder to make a mess of things if you are here now. To be here now, it requires solid, repetitive practice. You will have to really work on it, especially in this animated American culture. No better reason for meditation exists than to find the holiness of the present moment.

Eventually, we all swim in the same river. You understand? Anything you do will someday affect me in some way. We are all downstream from one another and ourselves. When we mess up the river here, we'll get back in the river tomorrow and be swimming in our own mess.

Let's work together. If we work on our actions today, the reactions will be beautiful. This is how we help future selves and help add more love to the whole world. Remember my friends, all we carry is the Karma we create. Let's commit together and do a better job.

Ok, everybody, thank you very much and have a good night. Please, let's bow together now, ok?

"Thank you, Bhante."

CONTEMPLATIONS

———

*Don't let your heart become blind by relying
on your eyes to see beauty.*

WHERE DOES THE APPLE COME FROM?

———

Story 4

Hi, everybody, how are you this evening?

"Hi, Bhante!"

Most days, my feelings are not good. I don't know what it is, maybe bad Karma from another lifetime or something, but no matter what I have to handle it. I am sick a lot, and sometimes driving myself is too much for me. In Sri Lanka, monks don't drive at all, so I am used to asking people for help.

One evening, I asked one of my students to drive me to my meditation class in Chicago. He arrived at the temple late. I could tell he was embarrassed and felt bad. I knew how to handle this situation as I have managed people's emotional reactions, especially around monks, many times. They often start to blame other people and outside factors. I understand because I used to do the same thing. Taking responsibility for our actions is hard work. Part of our daily practice has to be to work on getting to the root causes of our suffering, and most often the only person at the root of our suffering is ourselves. This is a great thing to remember—we create our situations by how we react to them.

When we got in the car, right away I could tell we were in trouble. He was angry at all the cars that got in our way. So often when you are most in a hurry, it seems the world is set up to slow you down. But if we had not been in a hurry, we wouldn't have even noticed the traffic and would have enjoyed our time together. When we got onto the interstate, the highway was full of big trucks. Almost as soon as we got into the fast lane, a big eighteen-wheel truck turned in front of us, slowing us down again. My student blew up in anger, screaming that he hated that truck driver. His mindfulness was totally gone. Traffic became so heavy we had no choice but to surrender and go with the flow. As my student's anger grew, I thought about what I had to do.

"What are you eating right now?" I asked my student.

"An apple," he responded angrily. "What do you see on the side of that truck that just cut us off?"

"Apples."

"So what kind of truck is that? What are they doing?"

"It's a produce delivery truck."

I was quiet again before continuing. "So, they are bringing food to the people, right? And maybe that driver delivered the apple you are eating right now, right?" Right away, I could feel his anger starting to go away, just a little bit. I continued. "Here we are going to teach people meditation and how to practice loving-kindness and to show them how to practice generosity, and at the same time we are being angry with the driver of that truck who is delivering food to people. How can we do both of those things at the same time?"

I watched his face. He understood right away what was happening.

"I understand, but I don't know how to do this when you are not around to show me. I struggle with this a lot," he thoughtfully responded.

"My friend, let's together right now follow our gratitude for those apples all the way to their roots. I am going to ask you some questions."

"Okay, go."

"Who filled that truck with all those apples?"

"Probably some dock workers somewhere at a distribution facility."

"Okay, let's extend our gratitude for their hard, noble effort, we are so grateful to them. Without them, the people who will be fed couldn't eat, right?"

"Right."

"Who got the apples to the loading dock?"

"Probably another team of workers who move them from picking crates and clean them and get them ready for delivery."

"You got it. Let's now extend our gratitude to all those workers for their noble effort, we are so grateful to them, too, because without them nobody can eat the apples, you understand?"

"Yes, I understand what you are doing Bhante, I get it now. You made a great point."

"Let's keep going, we are not done. How did the apples get into those picking crates? And who built the crates to hold the apples? And who built the ladder that the pickers stood upon to pick the apples? And who fed and housed the pickers so they would be strong and healthy enough to do their job? And who took care of the apple tree so it could grow those apples? And who planted the seeds of the apple tree? And who got the dirt ready for the seeds to be planted? And who cleared the land first to make room for the growing fields?"

By the time I was done going back to the root of our appreciation, we had arrived at our meditation class, and my student had forgotten all about his anger. He realized how much we have to be grateful for and how deep our appreciation can extend when we go to the root of gratitude.

This is true for each one of us. When we lose our mindfulness and we can't handle the present moment, I think it's a great benefit for ourselves and our whole world if we do this root gratitude practice. You can do this anytime, anywhere, with anything. Think about how much further we could have gone being grateful for those simple apples. Someone built that truck, someone built the road the truck drove on, someone risked their lives for the oil for the truck. The list almost never ends, right? We are all connected. We all are participating in some way in almost everything that happens. It is so important for us to remember.

Ok, everybody, thank you very much and have a good night. Please, let's bow together now, ok?

"Thank you, Bhante."

CONTEMPLATIONS

———

When you are truly honest, kind and moral,
all beings can sense it even before you speak or act.

ALL THE DHARMA WAS THERE

—

Story 5

Hi, everybody, how are you this evening?

"Hi, Bhante!"

One day, I was flying a three-leg flight from Arizona to Detroit to Chicago. I was already tired and frustrated from a hard day and hadn't realized I booked my flights this stupid way. When I am tired, my mindfulness becomes so much harder to find. You understand, yes? As we boarded the plane, a couple behind me was very loud and talking on cell phones. Everyone around them became angry from their behavior. The couple was so distracted, they didn't even notice how they were affecting others.

Once on the plane, I found my seat, hoping the whole time the couple would not sit near me. I am not tall, you know, so I always struggle to get my luggage up in the bin above my seat. Sometimes people see my robes and help me, or sometimes people see my robes and they hide, afraid to talk or look at me! It is so funny to me the different ways people respond. I do my best to make everyone feel comfortable. As I was struggling to reach the overhead bin, the loud, tall man pushed me out of the way and used his height to take my space for his and his wife's luggage. All my hoping that they would sit far away from me didn't work. They were my neighbors. In that moment, I felt anger come up inside me. I know that feeling so well. I felt I wanted to punch his face! When I was a young monk, my anger always was connected to a physical reaction. I struggled with it for so long and sometimes still do.

The reason we practice meditation showed up in my very next breath. The moment I noticed my anger, I also saw the opportunity to practice. I took a long breath, found a new home for my luggage, and made a strong determination to sit down and practice kind patience and acceptance. I realized all the Dharma was right there for me to study and work on. My ability to pause and not act on my initial feelings is the direct result of my spiritual practice. You understand what I'm saying? The Dharma is always here. In all situations. This is so important to realize. When you do, your life will get better.

As other passengers boarded the flight, the couple remained on their cell phones. They were so loud I felt like my seat was shaking. They were yelling! People became so angry, and as the plane took off, they still didn't get off their phones, so the flight attendants had to stop them. I was sitting in the aisle seat, she was in the middle, and the tall man was at the window. The moment the plane was up and service started, they both ordered wine. She was a very heavy woman and used some of my seat to fit. I could tell she was so uncomfortable, so I tried making room. The second she would get her wine, she would drink it and order another one.

This kept going, and I felt like she got louder and meaner with every drink. She could not sit still. She kept shifting and shaking and trying to get settled. The first moment we hit turbulence, she spilled her wine all over me and my robes were soaking wet.

My anger started again in my belly. I could feel it rising up in me. She didn't even apologize or try to clean up. I grabbed my napkins and was trying my best to just do my job and keep quiet. They started laughing at me, watching me try to clean myself, and still didn't say anything to me. Because her wine was gone, she grabbed her husband's wine and drank it all in one big gulp. He got so mad, I thought he was going to hit her. They started yelling and fighting.

In that moment, I felt so embarrassed. I was thinking about people I was about to see and the next class I had to teach right away after I got off the plane. I was thinking, "They will think I peed on my robes, or if they smell the wine, they will think I am drunk!" As soon as I noticed my embarrassment, I thought, "Okay, I have to stop this story right now! I am a monk. I have to handle this situation and use my practice." I picked up the book I brought, *How to Deal with Angry People*, and began reading until they finally quieted down. After a while, I put the book down and shut my eyes for a nap.

Soon the woman's elbow jabbed into my side, and she said, "Hey, I need this book!" She took it out of my hands and read the title out loud to her husband, *How to Deal with Angry People*.

I was quiet a moment, and responded to her, "Yes, you do."

She didn't understand, so I said, "You just told me you need this book, and I responded, 'Yes, you do!'" I gave her the book to keep, and we all laughed. In that moment, she became so grateful, and I realized again that the Dharma is always here. I realized this woman is my Buddha, my teacher. She taught me more than so many things I studied and spent time trying to learn. The Buddha shows up in so many moments, and I miss it often, but when I notice I am so grateful.

I got home after midnight, and right away I went to my bookshelf to find the sutra I'd been thinking about since managing this situation. I knew Buddha had taught about the five ways to handle annoying people. I quickly found it:

1. Practicing loving-kindness

2. Practicing compassion

3. Practicing equanimity

4. Forgetting and ignoring situations that don't serve us

5. Remembering people are responsible for their actions and Karma

Ok, everybody, thank you very much and have a good night. Please, let's bow together now, ok?

"Thank you, Bhante."

CONTEMPLATIONS

—

You will have to rely on yourself.
Teachers guide the way, friends give support, life is the opportunity.
How you do the work is up to you.

VEGAS STRIP CLUB

Story 6

Hi, everybody, how are you this evening?

"Hi, Bhante!"

I travel the whole world these days, teaching meditation and meeting new people. I am so proud about my life, no ego about it, I just really feel I am doing my best every day, and know I am helping lots of people. It's a blessing to do what we love to do and know it helps others. One of the places my trips have taken me back to many times is Las Vegas. This is a very interesting place for a Buddhist monk.

One evening in Vegas, I borrowed a car from one of my good friends to drive to my meditation class. As I was crossing the Vegas Strip waiting to turn left, I got rear-ended. I got out of the car to make sure the other person was okay, and right away, I could hear someone yelling at me. I was looking at her and smiling, and I asked, "Why are you yelling at me when you are the one who rear-ended me?"

She looked so young and was dressed in a tiny skirt. I felt right away something wasn't good about this situation. I completely trust my heart in almost all situations now. I think this is a result of living with a spiritual practice for so long. I almost never detour from what my heart tells me, and when I do, things don't work out good. We can all trust our hearts, they really do guide us, so one big job we each have is to learn how to feel and understand what our hearts want.

"No need to get mad at me," I tried explaining to her. "Let's share our insurance and go from there."

Immediately, she started to cry, and I could see she was shaking a little bit.

"I don't have any documents or insurance. I borrowed this car from my cousin," she explained.

"You have to get the insurance papers," I explained. "I am in the same boat as you, I borrowed this car, too, but still we have to own our responsibility and take care of it."

"If you want these documents you have to come to my work, all the documents are there," she responded. It was 9:30 at night. I didn't know where she was working, but I trusted my heart again. "Sure, I will follow you."

I followed her down the Strip. Eventually, she stopped in front of a giant building with flashing lights. Most of the buildings there are giant with flashing lights, so I didn't feel it was that unusual.

"Wait for me, I will bring them out," she said as she walked away. I sat parked in front of that building a long time. When I sit in a car, I look like a child—you know, my body so small. I saw people staring at me trying to figure out what I was doing there. Eventually, two big muscle men came to my window. I learned later you call them "bouncers."

"She is inside waiting for you. Come with us!" they said.

Again, I trusted my heart and walked with those men into the lobby. Right away, I saw girls sliding on poles, flashing lights, and giant screens with naked people on them. Naked dancers were on a stage, and I panicked. I started to sweat and thought, "Oh my, I am not in the right place for a monk."

I stood in the lobby in shock. My brain flooded with stories about what people would think of me and what a bad person I was for showing up here. But then my practice kicked in, and I watched my breath, and right away my mindfulness came to my head. I realized if I had wanted to come to a place like this, I would never have worn my robes, so people will know I am not here for trouble. I was scared and concerned, but I stopped the stories and held on to my mindfulness. This is one of the great benefits of practice. All the times we practice meditation when we don't want to, when it feels like it's not working, these are the moments it's for. Our practice can protect us long after we put in the time.

Soon I felt someone grab my hand and pull me into an office off the lobby. A man said, "I am very sorry. I could feel how uncomfortable you were. I know you are a Buddhist monk. I am the manager of this strip club, and I am so sorry we've put you in this situation." In the corner of the room was the young woman who hit me. She was crying so hard. When she saw me, she grabbed my hands.

"I don't want to go to the police, please help me!"

"Why, what is going on here?" I asked. Right away, I knew my heart had brought me and this poor young woman together for me to help her. The opportunity for me to do my job is always present. It's always available to you also, just look around. We don't have to help whole world. We have to just help the next person who shows up in front of us. Stop making big plans to help, stop worrying about big things, and just start helping whoever is here now in the present moment. This is only way I know to fix whole world. One at a time, you understand?

"This place, this is my job. I am a dancer here. I am desperately trying to make money. I am pregnant."

I guessed her to be maybe nineteen years old, and I saw my sister and my mother and all the woman in my life deep in her eyes. I offered her the same level of compassion I would my mother—there is never any real difference—so I decided to not go to the police or involve her any further. Before I left, she gave me her contact information.

When I got back to my friend's home, I was so nervous to go inside and tell them what happened to their car and about the strip club. They burst out laughing so hard. "Don't worry, Bhante, this is why we have insurance. They will fix it, this is no big deal at all, and hearing this story is worth any cost to fix the car!" Moments like this, I saw my friends' practice in action. The ability to laugh, to be easy and trust that all is well. To not get worked up about things, to remain calm. These are wonderful qualities of the practiced person.

"Bhante, if you go again, please let us know and take us with you!"

"What? Why?" I asked.

"We want the Buddhist monk discount for the strip club!"

The next day, the insurance called me. I explained the whole story again, and we began talking about my work. He was so interested in learning about meditation. We developed a friendship. He joined me at meditation classes, and we now have a connection we would never have had without that accident.

Shortly after, the young woman called. Her life was such a mess, and she said she liked talking with me and appreciated my kindness. I learned about her life, and we talked about meditation and how she could use it to help her life get easier. She asked for spiritual assistance, and I knew again my heart was the right thing to trust. You learn this too, it will really help. It doesn't matter who we are. It doesn't matter where we go. It doesn't matter what we do. We always meet people in our lives who need our compassion and kindness. We are all human beings. All that matters is, how we handle the situation in front of us? How do we care for one another? In every moment I find my gratitude to the Buddha who gave me this simple practice:

1. Think wisely

2. Act compassionately

3. Live lovingly

This is all I need. All you need. If we never work on anything else in our life, these three simple tasks are enough to change the whole world. I really believe this.

As you leave tonight, please ask yourself, are you in that practice? If not, start today.

Ok, everybody, thank you very much and have a good night. Please, let's bow together now, ok?

"Thank you, Bhante."

CONTEMPLATIONS

———

Love is only a word until it is put into action.

CONTEMPLATIONS

THE SHOEMAKER

Story 7

Hi, everybody, how are you this evening?

"Hi, Bhante!"

Tonight, I want to talk with you about giving. Is giving easy? I don't think so. We say it is, but if it is, with as many people as there are in the world, how come anyone remains in need? It's not easy, especially material things. Beyond words, when we get to the actual moment of giving, we hold it. We ask a thousand questions. "Why am I giving? Is this sincerely needed? Is this worth it? Are they worth it?"

We must give. All the questions just get in the way. Buddha's teachings are so simple and clear: no giving, no practice. If you don't know how to give, there is no spiritual journey. Buddha said something like this, "Once you know the power of giving, you will never use the things you have without sharing." I am lucky. Coming from my poor village where giving is the culture, I always feel I want to give, share, and support other people. If I don't do it, I feel something in my life is missing. I can't live with myself or my actions. I feel unfulfilled in a way that makes my life not work. As a practitioner, I am always looking for opportunities to give and share. It brings so much joy to my life.

I once had an amazing job teaching for "Semester at Sea." I was traveling in Peru with college kids, and we went on an excursion together. While they were shopping, I was resting along the roadside waiting for them. Across the road from me was a man, a roadside shoemaker. I guessed he was in his mid-fifties, and he looked so tired and hopeless. I couldn't stop looking at him, and I could feel something inside me bubbling up. My instinct said, "Give something to this man." As a monk, I don't always carry money, and I had left any little money I had with my travel partner. When he returned, I asked him for my twenty dollars. He immediately started the questions. "Why are you giving money to some random guy on the roadside that you don't even know?"

I was quiet and let his questions pass before I responded. "No questions. Let's just give unconditionally."

"What's going on here?" the other students asked as they returned and saw us debating. "I have been watching this man while waiting for you all, and I really feel I want to give to him. I feel he needs our support in some way. I am not sure, but I know I should trust this feeling."

They all began questioning me, challenging me. "Why would you give him something without any service from him? What's he done for you?" I realized right then, this is why people are still in need. The clinging to right and wrong we all have, the belief that exchanges need to be equal, this stops us from action.

"Sharing is essential to our spiritual practice. All your questions can't be answered, but what I feel in my instinct, in my heart, I know it's right. You all need to learn to trust the feelings in your heart more often. I think we all have them, but we don't all notice. Spiritual practice is to begin noticing and to begin acting on them without question."

We all sat on the roadside quiet. One of the young students handed me his ten dollars. Then another one pulled out his wallet. Soon, each student contributed to a little pile of money. We all walked across the road, and I asked the shoemaker about his life. Part of giving is listening and caring. "I am the only person in my family who works," he said with tears in his eyes. "I have three children in school, and every day I come here to work and feed my family. Some days I make a few dollars, and some days I make nothing, but I'm here trying my best." I could see the pride and suffering in his eyes. I was so happy I had trusted my heart. "Every day I live with fear wondering, how am I going to feed my family?"

When we handed him our sixty dollars, his face lit up with surprise. "How did you know I didn't make any money today? How did you know I needed this so badly?" he said with tears rolling down his face.

"We are all human beings. When we become deeply connected from heart to heart, we can hear and we can see and we can feel each other. I felt you needed help. Don't wonder anymore, just enjoy our gift."

What I am asking you all tonight, be sensitive. Feel other people. Take time to look into other people's eyes and feel their heart. Listen for what they are telling you without words. Do whatever you can to help people and remember, no giving, no practice!

Ok, everybody, thank you very much and have a good night. Please, let's bow together now, ok?

"Thank you, Bhante."

CONTEMPLATIONS

———

*Every moment we are losing
whatever belongs to us.*

THE
MEMORIAL SERVICE

———

Story 8

Hi, everybody, how are you this evening?

"Hi, Bhante!"

A while ago, I don't remember how many years now, one of my good friends passed away. She was in a car accident. I knew her and her brother, and he invited me to speak at her memorial service. I was honored to support him and say goodbye to my friend. Her brother was my student. He and I studied together for a long time. When we would meet, he would always talk so negatively about his sister. "She's terrible! I am so tired of dealing with her issues! I just hate her!"

As I sat in the service, one by one each family member got up to speak, telling stories, laughing and crying. The memories of my friend were so beautiful. When my student got up to speak, he was so emotional. He talked the longest of everyone. "My sister was the best sister ever. She was my best friend." The more he talked, I was thinking, what is real? He had talked negatively about her for so long I couldn't understand what had changed. Since then, I have learned that after a death of someone we love, we often regret how we behaved while they were living. I wonder if this might be as common as the experience of suffering. This experience has helped me behave better while people are living, and sometimes I even reflect on what I might regret if they were gone, and this helps me be kind in the present moment.

After the service, another friend drove me home and said, "Bhante, you did a great talk." I shared with him how confused I was about my history with this brother and sister and how much they had hated each other, all the things they had each said about each other. I was upset. I had not experienced or noticed such differences before."

Bhante, one day you will die. I will be overwhelmed with sadness. I can't think of a world without you, but I know it's going to happen. Instead of waiting like that brother did, let's ask each other right now, is there anything I can do for you when you die?"

"After I die, I won't have any needs. But on the way home there is a Thai restaurant, how about you take me there now!" I responded. We laughed, and I continued, "It is important what you do with me while I am next to you, not when I am dead. Same for me with you and everyone I meet. This experience today has been so helpful to me. I am going to make a strong determination to really be with people when I am with them. Smile, laugh, fight, again love, again laugh. We have to be real with people while we are right here. Good or bad, accepting life is all those things, let's work to be grateful in each moment we spend together." My friends' memorial taught me so much. I realized quickly how important being true is. Quality is important, not quantity.

We drove to the restaurant in silence mostly, then my friend said he still wanted to do something in my memory after I die. "Of course, you can do so many things! If you really want to do something for me, in my name, please plant as many trees in this world as you possibly can. That way even after I die, I am still helping people breathe, to be alive."

Ok, everybody, thank you very much and have a good night. Please, let's bow together now, ok?

"Thank you, Bhante."

CONTEMPLATIONS

Do everything without expectation,
then witness as you receive everything you need.

CONTEMPLATIONS

THE OLD LADY
WHO LIVED NEXT
TO THE TEMPLE

———

Story 9

Hi, everybody, how are you this evening?

"Hi, Bhante!"

I moved to the monastery when I was eleven to become a monk. I wanted to go sooner, but it took me long time to convince my parents to let me go. I am their only son, and this is big deal in my country, because sons take care of parents and family. When I became a monk, these duties went to my sister—monks serve the whole world, not just personal family. Soon after my arrival, many young monks were living with me. We were always fighting and running and climbing on trees like little monkeys. We were just like normal kids: crazy and loud and getting into trouble. I got in the most trouble.

Out back we had bath stalls. We would throw water on each other and fight and scream because our teacher wasn't nearby. On the other side of the temple wall was a neighbor's house. They were a very devout Buddhist family. They helped the temple, caring for the monks and delivering food and offerings of dana (generosity). There was an old grandma in that family. She was very strict. When we made noises, she would lean over the wall and yell at us, "Little monks, you need to be quiet! Take your showers and don't make such a big mess!" We didn't like her at all. We thought she was so mean and rude and arrogant. It was kind of a local story in our village, how mean she was.

But over the years, as I matured, I began to make a good connection with her. I could feel her love and compassion behind her words and angry face. She practiced every day at the temple. She was always there, always generous, always helping others. This was her entire life. As we grew up, she got so old. My teacher called me one day to say she was on her deathbed. I had already moved away, and I lit a small candle for her in honor of all her good deeds and remembered how scared we were of her. I realized then how often we judge people on the surface and not on their inner character.

After her death, my teacher called again to say she had passed, and he shared with me the last moments before her death. Invited to her house for the last ritual, he was chanting and blessing for her, this is what monks do in our culture. Her children were so sad, trying to say their final goodbye to their mother. She sat up to speak to her family, "Don't be sad, my dear family, this is life. Face the realities of this life. You can do it. The most important thing is, be mindful of what you do right now. You know the Dharma. You know the practice. Use the practice for your salvation. With the practice, you will never need anything else." My teacher kept chanting, and she was holding her palms together very mindfully and lovingly. At the end of his chanting, she bowed to him. "Sadhu! Sadhu! Sadhu!" (Excellent, excellent, excellent), she responded in appreciation. Then she passed away.

I often think about her. How beautiful her life. Sometimes people look mean, but who are we to make judgments of good or bad? Dharma will protect us all far better than our emotional judgments of others.

Ok, everybody, thank you very much and have a good night. Please, let's bow together now, ok?

"Thank you, Bhante."

CONTEMPLATIONS

Love is not fake, people make it seem so.

CONTEMPLATIONS

WHAT IS THE DHARMA?

Story 10

Hi, everybody, how are you this evening?

"Hi, Bhante!"

"I have a question for you. What is the Dharma?"

"Life the way it is."
"Nature of this life."
"Mental phenomena."
"Mental formation."
"What the Buddha taught."
"Truth." "Four noble truths."
"Eightfold path."

Yes, yes! These are all good answers. I've asked this question in my talks all over the world, and I get so many interesting answers. None of these are wrong, I just like to add to the list: I am the Dharma, you are the Dharma, nature is Dharma, air is

Dharma, not existing is Dharma, no Dharma is Dharma. I know it's hard to understand how one word can be so much. To help you understand, I want to tell you a story.

A man went to a very famous meditation center in Europe to practice. He had been saving money and planning the time for more than a year. It was called "A Loving-Kindness Retreat." He enjoyed the first evening. However, when he woke up the next day, he was so sick. He couldn't breathe very well. He had no energy at all. He tried to go to the meditation hall but found he couldn't even get himself out of bed. All day he was lying in his bed in his meditation hut. Not one person came looking for him. That evening, he heard the meditation bell was ringing to let the practitioners know the practice was starting. He heard some steps going by his room.

"HELP!" he yelled out. "Help, help!"

A man stopped and asked, "What can I do for you?" He sounded frustrated. The sick man asked for some warm water, something to drink."

I am so sick. Please, can you help?"

The man responded, "I am sorry, I don't have time to help you right now. I worked very hard to get to this retreat, so I can't miss any moment of the loving-kindness meditation."

Okay, everyone, I'm going to stop this story right here. I don't need to go any further. Did you get the Dharma? How many times have you missed the opportunity that was right in front of you? We get so focused and attached on one thing that we miss what happens along the way. This man was going to practice loving-kindness and missed the chance to actually be loving and kind. We all do this. We get lost heading somewhere, and we get so worried about getting back to what we planned that we miss the beauty and lessons of where we are and what happens in the present experience. We read so many books about meditation instead of actually practicing meditation. We recycle our old containers, but we don't work hard to use less of the world's resources at same time. I do this lots. I want something so bad, I get blind to all the other things I might get along the way. This feels like an epidemic in our culture, forgetting to love our current moment. We forget that each person is our teacher. I once heard a man talk about how to find love, and he said something so beautiful: "You are always just one hello away."

Ok, everybody, thank you very much and have a good night. Please, let's bow together now, ok?

"Thank you, Bhante."

CONTEMPLATIONS

---

*Loneliness is challenging but the moment you feel the beauty of it,
you no longer depend on another human being.*

CONTEMPLATIONS

EGO IS A SILENT KILLER

—

Story 11

Hi, everybody, how are you this evening?

"Hi, Bhante!"

I am a monk from a poor village in the tiny country of Sri Lanka. My house had dirt floors, my parents' house today might still look like a hut compared to what many are used to seeing in America. Because of my childhood, my world view was insulated by culture and tradition. A monk's life in a Buddhist country is so different. Thousands of years of tradition establish how we are treated and the life we live. Monks are so respected that, even as a very young boy, my parents bowed to me. Just stop for a moment and consider what that might do to you and your sense of self? Can you imagine?

In 1989, I was offered an opportunity to leave the country. When I accepted, I was twenty-one years old. For the first time, I left my village, my temple, my teachers, and my family. I was so curious and enthusiastic and sure of myself. I don't remember having any fear. Today I know how helpful fear can be, how fear is a doorway to look inside and learn what is going on. But as a young man, I wasn't connected to those experiences yet.

I moved to a temple out in the countryside of Brisbane, Australia. It was a converted farm house, and the facilities were very sparse. I was totally by myself for the first time in my life. Since age eleven, I lived dormitory-style with lots of other monks at a busy neighborhood temple. We always had people and activities and jobs to do. Living on this farm, I was so bored. I did my best, but soon I felt like an animal in a cage.

I woke one morning and was thinking, "I cannot live like this. I have to see what is happening in this country!" I had noticed a white bus going by at the same time every day. The signboard said "Brisbane City," and I decided I would go explore the city and enjoy the bus ride. I wanted to see my new country and meet people and feel alive again after so much time alone.

As the bus approached, I was so excited. My conditioned mind was still living in Sri Lanka where if a monk gets on a bus, no matter how many people are on, we get a front row seat out of respect. I didn't know to expect anything different. I was so used to this kind of holy life, living on a pedestal, I didn't even know another life existed. I stepped on the full bus and stood at the front waiting for the people to move, to give me their seat. It never occurred to me they wouldn't. They didn't even stop talking or notice my arrival.

The bus started to go, and I just stood waiting. Everyone began looking at me. Soon I felt they were all laughing at me and at my robes and my uncertainty of what to do next. I felt so hurt and angry. I decided right then, these people are all bad people, this is not a good country, and this is not a good place at all for a Buddhist monk. I didn't enjoy the bus ride at all and didn't enjoy any of the things I'd set out to do that day. My entire experience was ruined by my belief in how I should be treated, what I deserved, and what was wrong with other people. When I returned to the temple, I called my teacher in Sri Lanka. "I am done! I want to return to Sri Lanka right away. Please send me a ticket, I am done with this place!"

My teacher didn't react to my feelings, he just quietly responded, "Don't worry, I will send you a ticket. Just wait for it." I waited and waited. The mail came and went and no ticket. The days grew even longer. I soon began to think about what was happening. I asked myself questions and would spend the day walking, looking for answers in myself and the Dharma. "Who am I? What am I? What am I doing? What is my identity?" I had a thousand questions arriving in my mind every day. In this country, I felt I was nobody. I was too young to understand at the time that feeling "I am nobody" is a really good thing.

The longer I waited, the more I became hurt and disappointed. Then more questions around my hurt arose. "Who is getting disappointed?" I began to see my attachment to my identity as a monk. Slowly, I began to see I had a really big head about myself. My identity was so important to me, I missed all the other beautiful things happening around me. I studied the Dharma a lot those days. It helped me feel better. It still does. Whenever my heart hurts, the Dharma always helps. I searched the sutras to understand the truth from the Buddha on the one question that kept coming back up: "Who am I?" According to the Buddha's teachings, "I" means false belief, believing something that does not exist. We use "I" for our convenience. There are two different truths according to Buddhist wisdom:

1. **CONVENTIONAL TRUTH**: things we name or label for our convenience. Like a chair, a desk, a house. These are labels we put on things. That is conventional truth, you understand?

2. **ULTIMATE TRUTH**: understanding there is no such thing as conventional truth. Everything is impermanent, subject to change. Being in this impermanent world, we cannot have expectation that things will be as they were. Otherwise, we suffer. That is why I was suffering. I didn't know how to let go of my old experiences and expectations. I didn't know how to not be "I."

My ticket never came. My teacher must have known this time would help me deepen my practice. I soon began to see that ego is a silent killer. My ego killed my joy, my experience of adventure. We don't know it is killing us. To see that process of silent killing, I believe we have to closely observe and go deep, see the roots of what is fueling us and our feelings. We have to dig the root out. Taking the root out is not easy, it takes time. It takes a rigorous inward practice of meditation, contemplation. It takes teachers and noble friends and a spiritual community. Be patient. Keep digging. I did it. You can do it. Freeing yourself from the roots of ego and identity, letting go of expectation of how you think things should be and accepting things as they are, I believe this is the cure for all suffering."

Ok, everybody, thank you very much and have a good night. Please, let's bow together now, ok?

"Thank you, Bhante."

CONTEMPLATIONS

———

Life is simple; do not harm yourself or others.

CONTEMPLATIONS

NO TIME TO KILL

—

Story 12

Hi, everybody, how are you this evening?

"Hi, Bhante!"

My thoughts on what to say this evening are formed by people's questions and treatment of me. I can see the confusion and separation caused by believing we are so different from one another. I want you all to know that I am a real man. Sometimes these robes and my monkness can be confusing to the people. You seem to think I am better than you somehow. I bleed. I cry. I feel. I have good days and bad days. I am no different than you. I have problems and suffering and joy and desires. I have to practice, too. I make mistakes often, and every day I have to recommit to doing better. I have to really work my practice hard to make my life better. I want you to know this because I want you to believe me. Believe. Is this right word? My English not good, you know.

The word "believing," what I mean is this: if I can do something, you can do the same something. You and me, no difference, do you understand? It feels like the whole world knows me now. I am sort of a famous monk, people say. No ego about it, I've just been around a long time doing good works. I have met with maybe hundreds of thousands of people, and it is so funny, they all think they know me, even if I don't know them. We meet for a few moments in a Dharma hall, or they listen to me on YouTube, or they read "My Wish." I observe how many people I have been with, and I keep thinking it would be more helpful for them to see my humanness. Maybe then they could be more compassionate to themselves. I really want this for you. My only real job is helping the people. Every day that's what I try and do. I think I do a good job, I don't know, but for sure I do my best.

People think meditation is the only way to gain wisdom and happiness, but it is not. There are three ways to gain wisdom and happiness. The most popular one is meditation, but it is not enough. The three are:

> 1. Listening: in and out. I had first to learn to listen inside me, then outside me. The order of this is important. Many people get good at the outside and forget about the inside.

> 2. Thinking: thinking means when a situation happens, have selective thinking. Select what you are going to think. Only when you think clearly can you have wisdom.

> 3. Meditation: This is popular now, but many people practice without the first two. People think that by sitting and meditating everything is solved. It is not. You must have all three things to gain wisdom. What are the three again?

"Listening."

"Yes, yes, you got it. And another?"

"Breathing?"

Not exactly. Many people think breathing is part of practice, it is not. This is stupid. Don't misunderstand me, I'm not saying you are stupid, I'm saying this idea is stupid. You can't practice breathing. We have to breathe, otherwise, we die! Breathing is what we focus on, but it's always there. We don't bring our breath. All we do is bring awareness to it. We can choose to listen and choose to think and choose to meditate, but can you choose to breathe? Even if you think you can, you cannot. Your body will take over and do it for you automatically. Anyone else? What's another of the three?

"Thinking."

"Yes, that's it. And another?"

"Meditation."

Yes, yes. I try my best to do all three things every single minute. That way I can do a lot and communicate with people in a more helpful way. I can feel people and deal with situations very well. My productivity is higher because of it. Every day before I go to bed, I think, "Maybe this is my last sleep." I don't know what will happen tomorrow, still, today I did my best. If I made some mistakes, I refresh them, explore what I can learn and then determine not to do them again. If I don't wake up tomorrow, then who cares? I know I am clear. I did my best.

When I do wake up, I am always thinking, "I have brand new twenty-four hours. This day I do my best, to help myself and to help other people." As a result, I notice that life is beautiful. We can't have a guarantee how long we are going to live. When we understand that life is short, we become very positive, and we see the value of this life. We hurry up and try to do more good, be more wholesome, and practice more and more. Aware of the good this awareness brings, I don't want to use my time to consume nonsense, just sitting and doing nothing, killing time, those kinds of things. Sometimes people think I am, what is the American word, like alcoholic?

"Workaholic?"

Yes, workaholic. I think that definition of me is wrong. I like to work, yes, but it's not really work to me. I believe I am a servant to those in need. I know physically I am tired, but at the end of the day, whatever I receive with my mental practice leaves me feeling so content and happy. Every night when I go to bed, I don't have any regrets about my day. For example, today I helped so many children. Yesterday I helped children lots, too. I felt so happy about it. If I help even one teenager, one day they will think about it. When I come, they are so excited, they want to learn meditation. This fills me with joy.

If you want to enjoy your life and see the beauty of this life, what you have to do is see that life is impermanent. It is not a negative thing, it is the most positive, powerful experience we can have. The person who understands this, they are doing really well as a business owner, as a parent, as a human being. They know life is short, so they enjoy it, they have great family time, great personal time. I think the only way to do any of this is to practice those three qualities: listening, thinking, and meditation. That's what I do because no time to kill.

Ok, everybody, thank you very much and have a good night. Please, let's bow together now, ok?

"Thank you, Bhante."

CONTEMPLATIONS

———

Be simple. Think deeply.

CONTEMPLATIONS
—

THE RIVER

—

Story 13

Hi, everybody, how are you this evening?

"Hi, Bhante!"

Why do people make trouble in their lives? I think about this often. I listen to my students and study their behavior. The answer I have come to is, we all have boundaries, and we have attachments to what is not necessarily real but more like a feeling. We think things should look and feel a certain way, that people should act a certain way. We think things are only as they seem. I have found in this culture we run storylines about everything. It's hard to just accept things as they are. My mother and father are old now, needing much help from my sister and me. She does a great job, but still, she has her life and family and so lots of work. I could make so much worry and trouble in my life if I think into future a long way wondering how I will take care for them, how I will support them. And even more trouble if I think about what my culture expects of me as a son. However, if I stay present, what they need today is nothing compared to what they may need soon. But today, everything is handled. Worrying about tomorrow doesn't help them or me, it hurts us both. I have to let go of attachment to how I think it should happen, and what the world expects of me. Turning away from others' attachment to what they think something should be and checking in with myself and what I want and feel is hard but noble work. Nothing goes as planned it seems, especially with people aging. How I want them to live, how I wish they handled things doesn't change the reality. I have to just do my best and let go.

I clearly see being attached to what you think is real is a problem. People become attached to people, concepts, outcomes, and words. Attachment creates suffering. Even joyful attachment. An ordinary mind has boundaries. We have to practice and work to remove the boundaries our ordinary minds create. We have to work to let them go. If you really need something in your life physically, you have to learn to let go as a way to get it. In that letting go, we can retain what we have in a joyful way. It will mean more to us when we are willing to give it away. This is a deeply simple but hard practice.

There were two monks, a junior monk and a senior monk, traveling together. They came upon a river. There was a beautiful young woman sitting there scared to cross the river. The river was swollen and moving fast. The young monk said, "Sister, climb on my shoulders, I will carry you to the other side of the river."

Safely on the other side, the two monks continued their journey. "You are not a good monk. You touched a woman. You broke our precepts, our shared vows," the senior monk told the young monk. They were quiet awhile as they walked.

Eventually, the young monk responded, "Yes, I helped that

woman. I helped her by carrying her to the other side of the river and then sat her down in safety. Why are you are still carrying her?"

I think of those two monks often. When we hold on to things, we make them worse, bigger than they ever were. When we let things just be as they are, we enjoy the true reality of life. Buddha described his teachings as a raft, like a boat. He used the analogy of a man coming across a river. The man worked on the banks of the river to construct a raft. He worked hard and collected all the wood and made his raft and crossed the river. He was so happy he'd made it across and was so grateful to the raft he had built. He decided to take the raft home and keep it to remember his journey. When people asked about it, he said, "It is my raft!" and he became totally attached to this raft. This is the opposite of the teachings of the Buddha. If you build a raft, Buddha teaches us to leave it at the river bank and allow all other people to cross the river with your raft. Use it, love it, let it go. This is the essential teaching of the Buddha.

Ok, everybody, thank you very much and have a good night. Please, let's bow together now, ok?

"Thank you, Bhante."

CONTEMPLATIONS

———

*Death teaches us the importance
of being grateful.*

CONTEMPLATIONS
—

ONLY THREE THINGS

Story 14

Hi, everybody, how are you this evening?

"Hi, Bhante!"

Tonight, I have three small things to discuss with you. People come to the temple and come to talk to me about what is wrong in their lives, but almost never what is right and going well. Often, I help them discover how they participated in the problems that are occurring, and we talk about how to get better through practice and Dharma. I have realized, we have many tools for problems and sadness and the problems we create when we act from those emotional states. We have medicine and therapy and lots of books about what to do when things are going bad. But over time, I have observed something very interesting. We don't create any solutions for (or even recognize) the problems that can be created from action to positive things. Trouble comes both from negative and positive, and nobody seems to notice or be talking about this. I have realized, people create trouble from the positive things almost as often as from the negative. I have been thinking and studying the Dharma to come up with a way to help people be cautious of the good times, also, to find, live, and act from the middle path. Actions from exuberant joy or woeful despair yield the same problems if we don't have our practice. This is why Buddha always taught the middle path.

My first observation: be mindful to not hide pain with false joy. Our pain is so powerful and important. Hiding it helps no one. We need noble friends to help us, and we need to be noble friends. That means letting others in. Acting with false joy is like wearing a mask. We are stealing from our noble friends when we fake our joy. We are stealing their opportunity to be a noble friend. And we have no chance for real joy when we fake it. Pain leads to joy and joy leads to pain. This is reality, and so when we are authentic within each, we suffer so much less.

My second observation: don't lose track of mindfulness in the joy. When great things happen to us, we celebrate. When it is so sunny outside, and you are driving in your car with the windows down and good music comes on the radio, you feel a state of joy. You drive fast with wind in your hair. You feel free. In that state, if you were asked to make an important decision, everything feels possible, feels easy. You are happy to do it. You say yes, not paying attention to all your other responsibilities. In that free and joyful moment, you feel you can do anything. Then let me ask you something: what happens next morning? Now it is pouring rain. Your car won't start. No good music on the radio. It's freezing cold. Any commitments you made in that free and joyful place must still be kept. You quickly realize you are out of time. You said yes way too much. You can't get it all done now. It feels big and scary and impossible. We have learned to keep our mindfulness when we are sad, tired, and when we are feeling some kind of suffering. The same importance to mindfulness is necessary at the other end of the pendulum.

My third observation: watch exaggeration and ego. In our more joyful states, we begin to see things differently. Life looks bigger, brighter. We feel so good about ourselves. Pride swells up in us. When we interact with others during this time, exaggeration and ego begins to build. We believe in ourselves and our abilities a little too much. We stop listening to others, and we talk about ourselves. We describe life in an idealistic way. We begin to make stories.

These three observations are so simple. But not easy. I like to keep these three things in my pocket like change that jingles around as I walk. I need to be reminded all the time, in joy, neutrality, or sadness, that I must keep my practice. I believe if you never do anything else but work on these three things, your life will be so much better.

Ok, everybody, thank you very much and have a good night. Please, let's bow together now, ok?

"Thank you, Bhante."

CONTEMPLATIONS

—

There are no entities in the world.
There are only activities.

CONTEMPLATIONS

WELCOME HOME

Story 15

Hi, everybody, how are you this evening?

"Hi, Bhante!"

You all look at me tonight and see my robes and me sitting on this cushion in front of Lord Buddha in this Buddhist temple, and you think, he is a Buddhist monk. Yes, of course, this is true, but do you know what my real work is? Do you know what your real work is? What sits behind your job title?

I consider myself a furniture maker and house builder. My job is to build a beautiful house and design beautiful furniture and then invite all the people I can find to come into the house and take a seat. The house is our meditation practice, seeing the value of the pause and mindful observation. The furniture pieces I build are the teachings of the Dharma, the truth, the practical tools for daily living. Like a dinner party, I am the host. I greet you and open the door. I have made the food and arranged the rooms so everyone has a seat and can enjoy themselves. But I don't make you sit down on my furniture. I greet you and let you find your way.

I get lots of feedback about the Dharma I teach. People want me to walk them into the house and show them around. They want me to help them find a chair and then sit down with them in the chair. So many people say they only like the chair if I am sitting there with them. But this is not my job. Buddha said you alone must walk the path. My only job is to remind you and ask you, "Here is a path. Do you like this path?"

What often happens is, I hear the doorbell ring, and I go to the door, and you are standing there hungry and tired and ready to come in. Sometimes you've been circling my neighborhood a long time. You've seen my house, and you think it looks interesting. You are curious. You hear others talk about coming to my house and what they get from it. You are suffering and hurting and have gone to many other houses looking for relief. Eventually, you find my house, but you are too scared to come in. It's different. My house doesn't look like many other traditional houses in American culture. Eventually, your suffering becomes great enough that you overcome your fear and knock on my door.

No matter what, I have one promise to you and the whole world. I will always let you in. Of course, this is not really my house or my furniture, you understand. This is actually your house and your furniture. All that is here, you built. Now you just need to claim your spot. How? By allowing the Dharma to run your life. By committing to the truth. By helping your neighbor and extending loving-kindness every single moment you can find.

You just need to take your seat. Do it now. Find one, it doesn't matter which. Maybe it's a simple seat with only a few small lessons attached to it that you repeat over and over again. Maybe it's the seat that has a simple sentence as your entire practice repeated every day for the rest of your life, like, "May you be well, happy, and peaceful." Maybe your seat has ancient texts of all the wisdom teachers, and you study and translate them and really learn the body of the great teachers' works. Maybe your seat in the room is to simply take time out, to find peace in the silence, to grab a few minutes every day to let your mind rest. You may come back to this house a thousand more years, I don't know. But if you take a seat, suffering becomes optional and peace becomes possible, both inside you and around the whole world.

What I want to say to you all again and again is simple.

Welcome home.

CONTEMPLATIONS

——

Empty, empty. Happy, happy.

CONTEMPLATIONS

WISDOM IN ACTION

I've known Bhante Sujatha up close for half my adult life. This collection of stories you've just read, along with a thousand others still left to retell, have changed my life profoundly.

My actions, and the life that's emerged from them, happened as a result of using these core wisdom teachings in every aspect of my life. Here are a few stories of our adventures together that will give you a glimpse into our friendship and the influence of each of us on the other.

TAKING THE PRECEPTS

I made a sign one day on an old piece of wood, and I hung it above the doors to my meditation room. It says, "Enter the place you already reside." I entered there often. However, the place where I reside was harder to find. I didn't search far and wide. I had done that before. This time, I searched deep and narrow. I stayed and cooked and rooted around in the silence, in the crazy, in the pain, in the joy. Bhante Sujatha helped me understand that meditation can be all those things. Over time, the fruit of my earnest effort began to show up. I found a path—a set of principles, a peaceful home inside myself where I can always return. It was always there, waiting for me to access it.

Our world is on fire, in so many ways, and Bhante taught me the only choice is to start healing ourselves first so we are able to go into the world and help others. I am sure there is no way out but in, so in I go. I tried for a long time to find my own way. I've realized it's easier with a basic set of tools and guideposts such as noble friends and wise teachers to help us keep growing. With Bhante's urging, I decided a while ago to take the Five Precepts. They are so simple and straightforward to me, and I felt I was already living them, so I wanted to affirm my commitment.

The Precepts are a form of ethical practice like the

Ten Commandments of Christianity. However, as with most Buddhist traditions, they are only recommendations and only suggested as something to strive for if it feels right to you and if it's your truth. That's what I love the most about Buddhist teachings, the idea that you just take what you need, what feels right to you, and forget about the rest. Do the best you can, blow it, then try again. The Precepts are described many different ways. Thich Nhat Hanh prefers to call them the Five Mindfulness Trainings and I prefer that as well.

FIRST TRAINING

Aware of the suffering caused by the destruction of life, I am committed to cultivating compassion and learning ways to protect the lives of people, animals, plants, and minerals. I am determined not to kill, not to let others kill, and not to condone any act of killing in the world, in my thinking, and in my way of life.

SECOND TRAINING

Aware of the suffering caused by exploitation, social injustice, stealing, and oppression, I am committed to cultivating loving-kindness and learning ways to work for the wellbeing of people, animals, plants, and minerals. I am committed to practice generosity by sharing my time, energy, and material resources with those who are in real need. I am determined not to steal and not to possess anything that should belong to others. I will respect the property of others, but I will prevent others from profiting from human suffering or the suffering of other species on Earth.

THIRD TRAINING

Aware of the suffering caused by sexual misconduct, I am committed to cultivating responsibility and learning ways to protect the safety and integrity of individuals, couples, families, and society. I am determined not to engage in sexual relations without love and a long-term commitment. To preserve the happiness of others and myself, I am determined to respect my commitments and the commitments of others. I will do everything in my power to protect children from sexual abuse and to prevent couples and families from being broken by sexual misconduct.

FOURTH TRAINING

Aware of the suffering caused by unmindful speech and the inability to listen to others, I am committed to cultivating loving speech and deep listening in order to bring joy and happiness to others and relieve others of their suffering. Knowing that words can create happiness or suffering, I am committed to learn to speak truthfully, with words that inspire self-confidence, joy, and hope. I am determined not to spread news that I do not know to be certain and not to criticize or condemn things of which I am not sure. I will refrain from uttering words that can cause division or discord, or that can cause the family or the community to break. I will make all efforts to reconcile and resolve all conflicts, however small.

FIFTH TRAINING

Aware of the suffering caused by unmindful consumption, I am committed to cultivating good health, both physical and mental, for myself, my family, and my society by practicing mindful eating, drinking, and consuming. I am committed to ingest only items that preserve peace, wellbeing, and joy in my body, in my consciousness, and in the collective body and consciousness of my family and society. I am determined not to use alcohol or any other intoxicant or to ingest foods or other items that contain toxins, such as certain TV programs, magazines, books, films, and conversations. I am aware that to damage my body or my consciousness with these poisons is to betray my ancestors, my parents, my society, and future generations. I will work to transform violence, fear, anger, and confusion in myself and in society by practicing a diet for myself and for society. I understand that a proper diet is crucial for self-transformation and for the transformation of society.

The first time, I took the Precepts in private. I felt like it was a personal thing just between me and Bhante and a few noble friends that I wanted to have assist me in accountability. A year later, I felt compelled to do it in a larger group, as a renewal because my life improved so dramatically as a result of living this way. "Tyler, be a beacon to the world," Bhante kept urging. "Show people the power of the practice."

Several years after my first Precept commitment, I found myself in Sri Lanka experiencing a formal Precepts Ceremony. It became of vital importance for me to take the Precepts in Sri Lanka because I've come to believe this tiny little island, Bhante's homeland, contains the ingredients for what will save our world. That's really the only reason I was there, to cultivate in me the incredible spirit they have and, during a time when we need it most, to find ways to bring it to our Western world that seems so underdeveloped spiritually in comparison. Bhante, a few friends and I traveled to Anuradhapura, Sri Lanka and took our precepts under the sacred Bodhi tree, which many claim as the most historical Buddhist treasure in the world. For Westerners, especially from America, to come to this holy place and make this vow of ethical practice is most significant and an incredible honor for us and for the native Sri Lankans. Paying respect to these beautiful people who've been the keepers of this wisdom is the one of the most sacred acts we could do.

I've never been surrounded by so many people that are so deeply moved. Or so committed to the cultivation of an inner life. They came to witness, to celebrate and be part of history. Even the news media showed up, and we were on the 8:00 p.m. news for a few nights and got recognized out in public. Bhante escorted us through a processional of monks and dancers and a crowd of laypeople. We carried the cloth of a monk's robe, 360 feet long, along the parade route and to the temple where we then went in and requested permission from the chief monk to take the Precepts. Granted, we proceeded to the Bodhi tree where monks chanted and wrapped the base structure of the tree with the robe. As I walked, I was silenced in a way I've never been. I couldn't comprehend what I was seeing and feeling. I love witnessing such extreme love.

Our noble friends and monks had traveled hours by bus to join us, and we were literally surrounded by thousands of people full of joy, devotion, and commitment to what matters most. Later that night, I thought about how to express what had happened, what is happening, and I knew I couldn't. However, I realized I could represent through my daily actions what this has all meant to me.

I am responsible for the cultivation of wisdom and the practice of mindfulness in my own life.

Every day is my opportunity to add more love to the world by discovering the parts of me that can benefit others.

Every moment is an invitation for me to observe my breath and move to the middle path.

Within me is pure beauty and grace, and to express my gratitude for these treasures, every day I recommit to living the Five Precepts to the best of my ability.

Through the practice of loving-kindness towards myself and all living beings, I accept my responsibility to add more love to the world and will use all my actions to the benefit of humanity.

TRAVELING 10,000 MILES FOR A CUP OF TEA

Chanting from the temple next door woke me up ridiculously early. Bhante and I and our small group of pilgrims had been traveling for days, and I was desperate for a break. It was summer of 2014, and we were spending July in Sri Lanka when it's sticky-gross hot. I stumbled to the van to learn that our destination was way up in the mountains and required hardcore traveling by train, van, and foot via roads that looked like war. I decided this was my moment to bail. I took Bhante aside and announced that I wanted to skip, that I'd find a way to meet up at our next destination. He demanded I buck up and get ready, "I have an important lesson for you waiting at the top of the mountain."

Every inch of the day was only possible because of his dangling wisdom lesson that was sure to change everything. I'm a sucker for all things extreme. We traveled by train half the day through tea plantations and villages. The train was a royal blue with more than a hint of rust, and as we traversed through the most Ireland-green mountainside I'd ever seen, the vibrancy of the train's paint seemed to fade even more. I counted more shades of green than I knew existed. From my window, I looked out at the depths of poverty and at the natural majesty of our world. Seeing them so intertwined in the same moment was beautiful and devastating.

Rolling past rail-side villages where people brave a hard life in a big way, I watched in awe. Just a few hours into our journey, I peered deeply into the people's faces and saw a beauty in their efforts that humbled me. An ancient woman stood at one rail crossing, her arms folded, her gaze piercing and intent. She wore layers of fabric that contained every color my eyes had ever seen. A basket balanced perfectly on her head, and as we came to a stop, she exchanged fruit and nuts from her basket for rupees or well wishes—lack of money was not a roadblock in her business, her compassion was bigger than that. I took a picture of her that hangs next to me in my office so that I can be reminded to practice her level of compassion in all my affairs.

We traveled for five hours. A train load of humanity. Workers all focused on getting to the tea plantations so they can earn a living and produce a product for the world. Families being with each other. Sharing food. Laughing. Connecting. Nobody was texting or wearing headphones. They were listening to each other and smiling to the world.

The contrast between their lives and mine, and the realization of what went in to a simple cup of tea, the time and sacrifice required to deliver what appears to be such a simple product, I still can't reconcile it all. I shut my eyes now and see their blisters from sun, sweat, and extraordinary effort. My self-centered desire to see whatever the monk had to show me was the only thing that kept me going. I didn't prepare for a year and travel around the world to not get every single deep, spiritual lesson available to me. No matter how tired, Bhante's promise fueled me. "No matter what, just keep going"

We climbed 6,300 feet up to the very top of Lipton's Seat, and as we overlooked the tea plantations, mountain ranges, and endless blue, I waited for my lesson. I followed Bhante up the final footpath to the very top lookout. He handed me a hot cup, "Upasaka, (Male Buddhist vow taker) I've brought you all the way here to teach you how to drink a cup of tea." As we sipped our tea up on Lipton's Seat and looked out over the world, the wind blew the monk's robes so fiercely I thought he was going to parasail away. I grabbed on to him from behind and locked my feet into the fence, protecting us from the edge. He's so tiny that I could easily crush him. I felt proud for a moment, like I was keeping him safe.

"We must protect our minds like you are protecting my body right now," he said quietly.

"Monk, you really brought me all the way up here to reinforce the importance of compassion, mindfulness, and meditation, and you're using tea as the teacher?"

"I guess there are other ways, but I am a simple monk."

MAKING COMPASSION

One clock said it was just before 5:00 a.m. Another said 3:30 a.m. Back home, it might have been yesterday, today, or tomorrow, I had no idea. Time is an elusive bastard, and technology hadn't caught up to my travels, my body and computer each trying to sync into this new reality. It was a slow start. I decided sleep would need to accumulate. I wouldn't get it all at once. I hadn't now for days, instead I was relying on the hours stolen here and there compounding into enough energy. I think laying horizontally increases the fueling power of sleep and had finally found a way to lay down on a coconut husk bed at Bhante Sujatha's new meditation center, Sanatha Suwaya. Even the sounds of the jungle were no match for forty hours of travel.

When I woke to the sound of chirping, I headed to the small kitchen-like service area. I made coffee as the sun was rising above the jungle. I could hear the sounds of commerce waking up below us. Bhante Sujatha and this tall young monk named Damika came to help. As we talked, I had an idea. Bhante waited to respond and told me to be silent for a moment. Geckos burst into song, and I realized it was the same chirping that woke me up. His face lit up in a huge smile. "Our human minds are so cloudy and full,"

Bhante said. "We must wait for the geckos' pure minds to approve of our ideas with their song. If they are silent, our thoughts are faulty. This is what Sri Lankans believe." I was glad we had approval and smiled at the great commonality that no matter what you call it, God or geckos, many human beings rely on a higher power for clarity.Waking this early was unfortunate, we wouldn't sleep again till the end of tomorrow. That night, we were to begin our pilgrimage to Sri Pada, or Adam's Peak. We were a week early for high pilgrim season and likely would be alone on the trail, spending the night climbing what I'd heard described as 4,000, 5,000, or 10,000 steps, depending who you asked. What seemed generally decided was that it amounted to four miles of steps nearly straight up. As I described this journey, many people had asked me why I was going and what I was seeking. I had found I had no answer. My mind had felt empty. I had felt no longing for some big clarity or resolution, and as I had packed my bags, I had realized how incredibly fortunate it was that I would be arriving with no agenda.

English writer John Still described Sri Pada as "one of the vastest and most reverenced cathedrals of the human race." As we began our ascent, the pitch-blackness kept me from having any understanding of where we were headed or what I was getting myself into. The vast cathedrals John described were hidden from me. I am quite sure if I had seen them, I would have turned back. It turns out that the unknowing was the gift, and as I placed one foot in front of the other, I thought about how often we begin things without any real understanding of what it will take. Perhaps it's the naive mystery of things that allows us to proceed.

Several hours earlier, at around 9:00 p.m., we had piled

into the van. I had gotten everything ready: warm clothes, cold clothes, and various kinds of edible fuel. Bhante had brought nothing but his cloth monk's bag and robes. For a long time, I had been meeting with David, my trainer, four days a week. I knew my body could do it. Early on in the route, our faithful driver abruptly pulled over the van and jumped out and ran up to a street side temple. He got on his knees, bowing to the Buddha and then placed money in the donation bin. He was silent as he got back in the van. "He is asking for blessings of our safe journey, we do this every time," Bhante said. I could hear the geckos singing all around us. I didn't even wonder for one second if we were making a good decision to go.

I have no idea how we got to the beginning. Driving in the middle of the night, it had felt like an hour or more passed since we turned off any kind of main road. Some villages had maybe one or two lights. Many, none at all. When the van stopped, Bhante spread his giant smile and said, "Okay, let's do it. Time to make compassion!"

The locals don't say they are going to climb the sacred mountain. Instead, they say they are "making compassion," a locally universal term for the sacred pilgrimage. When I ask further, Bhante explains, "It's very interesting what happens as we climb, people's compassion just increases with every step. If you watch for it you will see. People don't talk, they just do. Compassion becomes actions. When one needs rest, everyone in the group just rests together. When someone needs water, another hands it to him. When one struggles, the others naturally lend hands. Together, as we climb, we make compassion. Making compassion on the mountain is easy, keeping it once we are done, that's the real work!" Maybe that is the point of the whole thing, I quickly realized.

A young man met us at the gateway to the base temple. The chief monk was away, but had arranged for him to escort us. I looked at his rubber Sri Lankan sandals in disbelief and tried to hide my specially-designed "ascending" shoes. It was 1:00 a.m., and the other monks were sleeping. When I asked our guide where we might see a leopard, he smiled and opened his arms wide saying, "All around us, my friend, they are watching!" I was happy, not yet realizing how dark our path would become. Bhante had a smirk on his face that told me I didn't know what was about to happen.

The tea huts were closed, the lights turned off along the trail. The stars and moon overwhelmed us. We seemed to be very alone on the trail. As we began our ascent, I could hear waterfalls all around us. The blackness hid everything, and I carried a flashlight torch that splashed a width of light maybe two feet to each side. Every sign was in Sinhala, Sri Lankan's native language, which I soon became grateful for. Not knowing how far we had gone, or had to go, saved me again and again. I never felt scared and never wondered. This was the first thing I realized as we kept going—the work is in the steps, and the steps are all you really think about. All the people who brought problems to ponder or issues to resolve must quickly realize that all that baggage will be unattended and burdensome.

Soon, I was surprised by the physical toll on our bodies, and as we walked, I thought about the ways people pilgrimage. Many are simply within—as states of mind and heart—but it's undeniable that the teachings from so many faith traditions describe the importance of physical pilgrimages. And as I stepped again and again, I began to understand.

Buddha said to undertake pilgrimages with a "devout heart," and I had worked on my body, mind, and heart in preparation. I've been on many silent retreats and various kinds of inward pilgrimages, but this felt very different. As the step size increased, and the slant of the path became more vertical, I began chanting our daily chant from the temple, from the Twin Verses of the sacred Dhammapada, "Mind is the forerunner of all states." I knew my body could handle this, I just needed my mindfulness to cooperate.

Buddhism places high value on sacred pilgrimages and describes them as deeply committed acts of faith that can be physically demanding spiritual practices as well as "inward journeys of the heart." In the Pali Tipitaka, the oldest surviving body of the Buddha's teachings, it says to try and make at least one spiritual pilgrimage in your lifetime. The pilgrimage is not really about destination, the journey itself is the most important part of the practice and, like meditation, the Buddha's teaching suggests pilgrimage as an opportunity to invest a significant dedicated amount of time concentrating on three qualities: Right Speech, Right Action, and Right Thought.

I did none of these three things—not even for one solid moment. The physical investment consumed me. As we rested at what was described as a halfway point, a lie designed to keep us from giving up, I was thoughtful for a moment about what I was doing on this path, mindful and a little sad I wasn't able to concentrate on the three qualities. Before we began again, I let it all go, reminding myself that true pilgrimage is an interior journey with the intent of training the mind and elevating the spirit. The path and destination are really the same, no matter where we are physically headed.

They say that the second half is significantly more trying on the body than the first half. The steps became more random in height and width, and in many areas, the incline was so significant I had to hold on to a railing and at times even crawl. Bhante had to be lifted on a few steps, his robes constricting him and his height working against him. Somewhere in the middle, I lost myself. My mind became more and more empty, the only thought was the next step. In walking meditation, we focus on the bones in our feet and we observe each of them moving. That observation—feeling each muscle, focusing on such a tiny thing—takes all you've got mentally. Continuing the climb felt just the same.

We talked occasionally, laughed, told stories. We stopped at numerous bluffs to catch our breath. It was perfect weather, and as we looked at the sky, the stars were magnified beyond anything I even dreamed possible. We soon discovered we were looking due north, toward India. I had no idea then what we were really looking at. The blackness stole the "vastness and reverenced cathedrals" from me, but we kept climbing, knowing something huge was about to be revealed. It never once occurred to me that we were hanging off the side of a mountain.

It never once occurred to me to think back to all the pictures I had seen. The only thing I thought about was the next step. This has become of utmost significance. I didn't even realize there was so much open space behind us. The darkness was so close, it felt almost as if we were in a tunnel. Hours later, my mind was blown as I realized how totally raw and exposed we actually were.

But I never once felt it. We just kept moving. More times than I can count, continuing a sacred commitment to keep moving was the only thing that got me anywhere. Step, step, step, step. If I had known, or even considered my surroundings, I'd have had a very different outcome. I could list a thousand things that only happened to me because I was willing to say yes: three steps, one bow, three steps, one bow. This pilgrimage was no different.

Very soon into the "hard part," the only option became to keep moving. Nearer to the top, we only made it maybe twenty stairs at a time.

Twenty stairs, rest.

Twenty stairs, rest.

As we climbed another twenty stairs, each one more slowly than the last, I thought about how many times I've given up on things because I couldn't keep the pace I originally started with and I marveled at what might have been if I'd not been attached. Twenty stairs soon became ten, but we kept moving. A sign, finally written in English, announced we'd made it to the last tea house and rest stop before reaching the top. The tea house was closed, but we reached in and stole a bottle of water each, committing to repay them on our way back down. The image of a monk "stealing" stayed with me and made me smile. At a ten-step rest point, Bhante pointed to a light. "That's it, that's the temple. We've made it." Saying we'd made it and actually making it turned out to be two very different things. The last sets of steps were as hard as the entire mountain.

I was soaked in sweat, and once we stopped climbing, I quickly felt like I was nearly freezing to death. I'm not sure if I was shaking from the cold or from the climb. After hours of feeling completely alone, I was surprised to see people already atop, meditating, sleeping, eating, laughing, and waiting. Lots of waiting.

We found a spot and settled in, as we were hours early for the sunrise. The temple monk would not awake for several hours to open the gates of the temple and let us in. Every day I get older, I rediscover that the top really isn't the top until you are in the temple, whatever your temple may be.

As we sat curled up trying to stay warm, maybe as many as a hundred or more pilgrims arrived. I had no idea anyone was behind us. The same scene repeated itself: they would arrive in t-shirts and shorts, so happy to have made it; they would go immediately to the temple gate and realize it's locked; and then they would look around and finally notice us all huddled up and waiting. Eventually they joined in, one after another adding themselves to us—individuals becoming part of the collective.

It would be embarrassing for me to attempt to describe the miracle of sunrise. The realization of where we were, what we had done, and what I was looking at came slowly. The slowness was mandatory, I couldn't have comprehended what I saw. I still haven't yet fully. As we waited for the head monk to wake up, I never once thought about the millions of pilgrims before us, or the sacred acts performed here, or the significance of this interfaith holy site at this particular time in our world's history. I didn't have one deep or profound thought—no insight, not even for a second. I've been told again and again, that's the entire point of a pilgrimage, to become that completely empty. I most certainly succeeded.

As the sun rose, so did the temple's monk. When he saw we

were traveling with Bhante, thank god for those robes, we were near the first to be let in. I was so captivated by the views, I had to force myself to notice anything of the temple site. We left our shoes at the gate, a moment that for me was the most significant of all. I am moved beyond anything I can describe any time I see people prepare for worship, and the sight of shoes outside any sacred space always blows me away. We were quickly escorted to the sacred "footprint," and Bhante and I got on our knees, bowed, and then began chanting. A woman and her daughter were behind us, and the mother began crying, being so deeply moved. I moved away, and her daughter took my place, bowing with Bhante. Then he did a special blessing chant for her.

We came upon the famous bell, the first to begin the procession of pilgrims. Bhante went first, ringing it fourteen times—one for each of his ascents to the sacred peak. His last pilgrimage was twenty-five years prior, and when he reached the bottom, he announced he would never climb it again in this lifetime. He kept his word for a long time. I'm sure glad he broke it for us. For me, noble friendship is defined in the reverberation of that bell. When I rang it, I realized just how resonant it was, and I am certain villages across the valley hear it constantly, a daily reminder of faith.

Only later, finally rested and clean and alive, did I reflect on all the people who had pilgrimaged to that holy site—Marco Polo among the notable. What's so interesting is how little all that means to me. Nowhere during the journey did I give reverence to anything other than my steps, to anything other than us continuing. We just kept going. For our final mountaintop moments, we recited two sacred passages directly from the

Buddha's teachings, and we lit candles and incense on an altar by the edge. We each made private vows. Mine were first, to know myself, and second, to allow you to know me. The second so much harder for me than the first. The backdrop of this ceremony was beyond comprehension. Another traveler took our group picture but there was no need to memorialize as an imprint. Like the sacred foot, it is now in my heart.

With anticipation to see how we had come there and to get back to rest, we began our descent. I naively assumed we'd make quick passage. We even began describing our desired breakfast orders, knowing full well our only likely options would be more rice and curry. Somehow the fantasy of waffles fueled us. Even before I'd gone down the first ten stairs, I began to see what we'd just completed. It was unrecognizable in the light of day, no similarity whatsoever even though we'd just traveled every step. In every way, the way down was the opposite of up—raw, vulnerable, hanging off the side of a mountain in a tremendousness I have never experienced. I immediately understood John Still's words, because I was standing directly within "the vastest and reverenced cathedrals of the human race."

I was reminded of our opportunity to "make compassion" as I watched us all manage each other with a grace and warm-heartedness I rarely see in a crowd. People of every degree were descending, and each had their own speed, need, and desire. I didn't witness even a single moment of frustration, within me or anyone else.

We explained to the Tea House owner that we'd stolen his water, and he happily accepted our over-repayment. As our bill was being settled, I stood near the edge and watched the pilgrims.

Nobody was headed up. Very few would make the journey if the effort required was this visible. I truly believe I would not have. I had never expected the flight down to be so much more difficult, but it was tenfold, and nearly destroyed me. Numerous moments had my legs shaking so badly I wasn't sure I could remain standing. Going down faster became easier than a slow walk, the momentum seemed to work on our behalf. I finally saw all that I had missed: Buddhist Temples, Hindu Shrines, Mother Mary. Sri Pada is in some ways not just a mountaintop temple, but also an interfaith holy trail. Each resting place offered spiritual and physical rejuvenation for her pilgrims.

Near the bottom, I discovered I was far ahead of Bhante and our group. My legs hurt so much by then that I couldn't stop descending. If I stopped, I almost couldn't stand. I found a small river below a bridge and put my feet in the water. It was then I remembered the sound of all the waterfalls I had heard in the night. They were all around me. I sat for a half hour or more, watching the people and listening to languages from all over the world. I smiled as I imagined what brought them here. "You never know about another person's true story, that is why compassion is mandatory all the time," Bhante reminds me often.

When we got back to the base temple, the monks were wide awake and had made a dana (generosity) meal for us. Traveling with Bhante Sujatha affords us the most unique experiences, and we were escorted into the temple where a meal was presented. We sat alone while they served us, the customary tradition in this country. "Guests in the house, God's in the house."

Walking from the base temple to the van, I anticipated a distance of maybe a city block. The night before, it had felt like we had just journeyed an easy ascending trail from our van to the temple. In the light, also known as reality, it was a hundred times further than I imagined. "We all put in such great effort to see things clearly, however it has its disadvantages," said Bhante. As I walked those final steps, I recommitted to just accepting the present moment rather than always trying to see more.

What I had thought was a tiny trailhead was actually a bustling village. There were tea shops and temples and small hotels everywhere. The high pilgrimage season was a week out, and all the shopkeepers were getting ready. I wondered how often they stopped to consider the love they were adding to the world by being in service to all who venture here. I suspect much like me, they don't think of it at all. The work, the next steps, that consumes them and the why is just an ego-filling distraction.

The van pulled away, and as we made our way through the villages, I realized what we had come through to get there. Humanity seems to go to great lengths to survive. Bhante took my hand and held it a long time. "I am so happy. All our problems are solved now." We rode in silence another moment before he said, "Empty, Empty, Happy, Happy." I had no idea then those small words would turn into a book.

"Just keep going," I thought—and maybe said—before I fell sound asleep.

WE BELIEVE

We believe in generosity towards others by any means possible.

We believe the true Noble Path is marked by generosity.

We believe that like humility, generosity is part of our true, authentic nature.

We believe generosity has many levels:

> think generously,
>
> speak generously,
>
> act generously.

We believe generosity comes from hearts that are fearless and free, willing to share abundantly all that is given to us.

We believe generosity lies at the heart of spiritual practice, and with practice our hearts will grow stronger and lighter.

We believe extending generosity to ourselves and others gladdens our hearts, is a direct way of healing division, and brings joy.

We believe that it's our obligation to generously add more love in the world.

We believe through generosity in all forms, the dharma and spiritual refuge will be maintained for generations to come.

RESOURCES AND CONNECTIONS

TO CONNECT FURTHER

To connect with Tyler and to read more of his work, head over to: www.tylerlewke.com

To follow Bhante Sujatha's travel schedule, or to see when he will be teaching in your area, check out his website www.bhantesujatha.org

For information on the Blue Lotus Buddhist Temple: www.bluelotustemple.org

MEDITATION AIDS

For a great meditation timer you can use from your phone, we recommend the Insight Timer app.

Tara Brach is a well-known western meditation teacher, author and psychologist, and she has podcast meditations and dharma talks you are sure to benefit from.

For a Buddhist path to addiction recovery and as a resource for down-to-earth dharma talks and meeting lists all across the country, check out our friends at Refuge Recovery.

RETREAT CENTERS

For information on our retreat center in Sri Lanka, please go to: www.sanathasuwaya.org

For a US-based retreat center, we love the work of the committed teachers at Spirit Rock.

BOOKS WE LOVE

My Wish, A Book about Bhante Sujatha, by Mary Gustafson.

The Heart of the Buddha's Teachings, by Venerable Thich Nhat Hanh.

Heart of the Revolution and all the other books out by our friend and renowned Buddhist teacher, Noah Levine.

All books by our dear friend, Bhante G, especially *Mindfulness in Plain English*.

ABOUT THE AUTHOR

Brutally irreverent and way too direct, Tyler Lewke finds himself in trouble often. He's an optimistic-pessimist, a grateful dad and friend, a business guy obsessed with making things work. Described by others as mindful and compassionate, Tyler is most inspired by helping people through the mucky parts of religion and spirituality to define a life of joy and service to others. Tyler believes there is "no way out but in" and that business and mainstream consciousness are here to stay, so he stands in the center of it all helping to transform things from the inside out.

Tyler was born months before the official end of the Vietnam War on the campus of Washington State University to a hippie mom and a heady scientist dad—a combo that has left him totally out of place in the mainstream. From an early age, Tyler knew he needed to make his own way and build things and businesses for himself. He deposited his last traditional paycheck at the age of 17 and set out to embrace mainstream culture and business on his own terms. Today, he is the unlikely CEO of a Midwestern company where he has transformed the culture from the bottom up by teaching how loving-kindness towards others and radiant happiness as a mission creates profit that can be used for good. Tyler's rebel approach and unrelenting work ethic—and his belief that capitalism and spirituality mix perfectly—have earned him a position at the top of his industry for two decades. His motto? Happy people. Closed deals.

At any moment, Tyler could be on a plane halfway around the world, high up in a tree, hiking the Pacific coast, or sitting in a board room in the Midwest redefining business as usual. "I love a million things. Tried the simple life and it's not really for me. I love business, I love big problems, I love drama and figuring stuff out. I see life as a Rubik's cube."

Tyler loves one thing the most: moving people. Their thinking, their hearts, their minds, their points of view and perspectives. "On this path, I think the only real key to happiness is to, no matter what, keep moving."

Tyler lives in the skyline of downtown Chicago, in a historic 150-year-old Victorian in suburbia, and from his backpack as he explores the world. He teaches meditation and mindful leadership and has written as a form of art and spiritual practice every day for as long as he can remember. He shares his personal stories of integrating a spiritual life into a daily mainstream existence through his blog, postsfromthepath.com, where he posts his raw, firsthand joys and struggles of trying to practice mindful principles in all his affairs. In collaboration with Bhante Sujatha, Tyler serves as president of the board for The Blue Lotus Buddhist Temple and Meditation Center in Woodstock, Illinois, where he and the dedicated Sangha work together to "promote individual peace of mind, compassion for all beings, spiritual growth, and an ethical way of life based on Buddhist principles."

Tyler thinks we all have only one real job: to add more love to the world.

ACKNOWLEDGMENTS

After not much deliberation, I've chosen to not name you directly in my offering of thanks for your amazing collaborative efforts on this project. Here's why. I attempt to live my practice by making choices measured against two questions:

1. What action will cause the most benefit?

2. What action will create the least harm?

To name you directly would inevitably cause harm. I would for sure overlook one of you who loved me more than I thought possible and played a vital role in this book. It's a guarantee that I'd mess up and then live with regret.

Within and beyond this project, in the countless ways we all need support, I'm humbled beyond words by your love and generosity. I bow to you again and again, and I transfer any merits earned here directly to you. I am terrible at asking for help, awful at receiving feedback and I tend to handle as much as I can on my own, often causing a great big mess. You have graciously overlooked my flaws and brought me your wisdom, guidance and support anyway.

You made all this so much better. You made me better. Allowing others to love us is a key benefit to this practice and one I keep learning. In this way, you were all my teachers, and I am grateful to you beyond measure.

Bhante Sujatha has taught me that I should give without remembering and receive without forgetting. I strive for this level of enlightenment and always come up short. But I keep trying.

Thank you. Thank you. Thank you. Especially you.